*50 inspirational true stories about faith under fire during the War Between the States*

By Michael Aubrecht
Foreword by Richard G. Williams, Jr.

PUBLISHED BY PATRIOT PRESS
Gettysburg, Pa.
www.patriotpressbooks.com



ISBN 978-0-9796000-1-2
Library of Congress Control Number: 2008920707
Nonfiction/Inspirational

First Edition: April 2008
USA
0 9 8 7 6 5 4 3 2 1

*This book is dedicated to my children, Dylan, Madison, Kierstyn and Jackson, as well as the rest of my family, friends and brothers and sisters in Christ. I would also like to add a very special dedication to my beautiful wife Tracy, who has blessed every day of my life.*

*"American history is our most cherished national treasure. However, learning about it means nothing if we can't adapt it to our lives today in some tangible, positive manner. It is my sincere hope that you will find these encouraging stories uplifting and apply the wisdom that they contain in your own life."*

Michael Aubrecht

# Contents

# Contents (cont.)

## King James Bible

All of the verses in this book are taken from the *Holy Bible, King James Version. The King James* or *Authorized Version* of the Bible is an English translation of the *Christian Bible* first published in 1611. The New Testament was translated from the *Textus Receptus* (Received Text) edition of the Greek texts, so called because most extant texts of the time were in agreement with it. The *Old Testament* was translated from the Masoretic Hebrew text. *The King James Version* has had a profound impact on English literature. The works of famous authors such as John Milton, Herman Melville, John Dryden and William Wordsworth are replete with inspiration derived from it. Although it is often referred to as the *KJV* (King James Version), particularly in the United States, the only active part King James took in the translation was lifting the death penalty attached to its translation and setting very reasonable guidelines for the translation process, such as prohibiting partisan scholarship and footnotes. Current printings of the *King James Bible* are based on an edition published at the University of Oxford in 1769, edited by Benjamin Blayney, and contain substantially the same text; however, there are a few differences between the 1769 and the 1611 versions.

# Preface

As a Civil War historian specializing in the role of religion, more specifically Christianity and its impact on the Southern Confederacy, I have always been fascinated by the positive stories that transpired during the darkest of times in American history. It has always been my opinion that, buried beneath the glorious and horrific tales of battle, hide the lesser-discussed stories of "faith under fire" that we can still learn from today. These lessons can then be affirmed through Holy Scripture.

In my first two books, *Onward Christian Soldier* and *Christian Cavalier,* I set out to present an intimate portrait of two of the South's most notable believers. My total "religious-focus," to an otherwise well-published subject, came about because I have always believed that there is much more to the legacies of these men than magnificent charges and legendary rides around the Union Army. I believe that secular historians have a tendency to focus on the battlefield actions and sometimes forget that there was more to their subject's character than just soldiering. Much more.

For example, the collective memory of General Thomas "Stonewall" Jackson is primarily one of a grim, ferocious warrior, whose steadfast courage and tenacity were tragically cut short by friendly fire. People recall his infectious bravery at the First Battle of Manassas, the brilliance of his Valley Campaign and the grand finale of his storybook career at the victorious Battle of Chancellorsville.

These are all very important events in the life of Thomas Jackson, but it is only when one examines his life *off* the battlefield, that they discover the story behind the man. Jackson's story is filled with the kinds of heartaches and hardships that would leave many of us questioning our own beliefs. It is a love story, filled with sorrow, testimony, hope and despair and a story that reaffirms the positive power of prayer. Ultimately, it is the story of a man who suffered greatly, but chose to embrace the will of his Savior as the foundation for a legendary life. Everything that followed was, in my opinion, a direct result of his religious experiences and convictions.

The same can be said about the story of Jackson's legendary subordinate, J.E.B. Stuart. Was Stuart "fanatical" in the pursuit of his faith, like Jackson? Probably not. But did religion play a pivotal role in his journey toward greatness? Absolutely. Stuart was a cavalier, but more importantly he was a Christian. He was, first and foremost, a man of faith, a man of duty and a man of devotion. His devotion was to his family, to his country and to his men. This was the "brick and mortar" of his character and, in my opinion, these admirable traits are what enabled him to rise to such legendary heights. By examining his lineage, upbringing and pre-war experiences, we can peer through the flashy red cloak and flowing black-feathered hat and see the real man buried beneath that magnificent cinnamon beard.

"Stonewall" and Stuart however, are two individuals who are part of a larger group of Christian soldiers. Their ranks include gentlemen such as Robert E. Lee, Nathan Bedford Forrest, the Reverend Tucker Lacy and others. My intention is to spotlight both the popular and lesser-known stories of these men. The title of this book, *The Southern Cross*, indicates a strong Confederate influence, but there are also stories from the Northern Christian contingency. These include Father William Corby of the "Irish Brigade," the "Angel of the Battlefield" Clara Barton and Union General Oliver Howard.

As with most works in this genre, each chapter covers a specific virtue and each page contains a relevant verse of Scripture, an associated quote and a short vignette on a related topic. I have defined five major categories that express the virtues of a Christian soldier. They are: *Courage*, *Duty*, *Faith*, *Honor* and *Mercy*. Each of these is illustrated by some of the most inspirational stories to come out of the War Between the States. There are forty of these uplifting devotions, as well as ten encouraging essays that address some of the subject matter in greater detail. All of them are religious in nature. I have included a special sermon that was presented to the soldiers in the field. This impassioned speech reinforces the power of the prayer warrior. A short biographical tribute to some of the South's most pious commanders follows.

As my previous Christian Civil War biographies were written to be both educational and inspirational, this book is intended to serve a much greater purpose. Devotionals are extraordinary works and the life lessons and scripture references that they contain can be reviewed again and again.

I hope and pray that the readers of this book will find something that touches them and stimulates a further interest in the reading of God's Word. This after all, is the foundation for the entire project, as well as my own prime directive. In fact, nothing would please me more than to know that someone put down my book and picked up the Holy Bible. Simply stated, the Lord has blessed me in so many ways and I want to share His grace and providence with you.

As a bonus, I have enclosed a wonderful study aid that will enable you to read the entire Good Book in one year from cover to cover.

Ralph Waldo Emerson once said, "Our best thoughts come from others." I fervently concur with this assessment. I have been very blessed to have some brilliant "others" in my professional life and I would like to express my humble gratitude to them for their contributions.

To Richard Williams, friend and author extraordinaire: Thank you for the wonderful words of wisdom that you have shared. They have made me a far better writer than I could have ever become on my own. To Gwen Woolf, my editor at *The Free Lance-Star*: Thank you for your generous mentoring and encouragement. If not for your belief in me, I may not have pursued this vocation any further. To Benjamin Smith and the good folks at *Civil War Historian* magazine: Thank you for your support and generous promotion of this project. To Chaplain Alan Farley, founder of the Re-enactor's Missions for Jesus Christ: Thank you for your dedication to spreading the Good News of the Gospel. Your focus on the Christian aspects of Civil War history has validated my own interests in the subject. Finally, I would like to add a very special thanks to my publisher Traci Lower and Patriot Press for believing in this title and doing a wonderful job in producing it.

Once again, I owe a very special debt of gratitude to my father, Thomas Aubrecht, who spent countless hours reviewing and proofreading my work, as well as to my mother Linda Aubrecht, who allowed my father to disappear for days on end, so that we could make our annual pilgrimages to the Hallowed Grounds of this great nation. I also want to thank my pastors, the Reverends Alan Hager and Mike Motsko of Spotsylvania Presbyterian Church. Their spiritual guidance was essential in helping me rise to the challenge of yet another book. Finally, I want to praise my Lord and Savior Jesus Christ, who makes all things, including this book, possible.

In closing, I hope that you enjoy reading this book as much as I did writing it. I welcome your comments, critiques and questions. I'd like to leave you with my own personal favorite, a bible verse that General Jackson was particularly fond of, and one that has become a daily affirmation in my own life, both personally and professionally:

*And we know that all things work together for good to them that love God, to them who are the called according to his purpose. (Romans 8:28)*

God bless.
Michael Aubrecht

# Foreword

The 20-year-old Confederate soldier swallowed hard as the noose was tightened around his tense neck. His heart felt as though it would pound out of his chest, yet he faced the last enemy with exemplary bravery for one so young. It was 14 October 1864 and there was a chill in the air. The events that had brought him to such a fate whirled through his mind's last moments as the bright autumn sun warmed his youthful face. Though his body was flooded with adrenalin, a calm peace slowly settled over his spirit and soul. Even his executioners looked on with admiration.

Albert Gallatin Willis had been serving with Confederate Colonel John Singleton Mosby's Rangers for several months. He relished the daring deeds of Mosby's raids and already had experienced several brushes with death. Earlier in the year, on February 18, Willis and James Foley Kemper had jumped from the second-story window of Parson Thaddeus Herndon's house barely escaping capture by Federals.

Though born into a wealthy Virginia family, Willis had chosen to pursue a life of gospel ministry and was at the time the war broke out, studying to be a Baptist preacher. Willis' thoughts drifted back to those days of studying New Testament Greek, when he had looked forward to the day he would be able to shepherd a small flock somewhere in the Virginia countryside, or perhaps a larger city church in Richmond or Winchester. Though he had not completed his studies, he thought how thankful he was now to know the God whom he would soon be facing.

Earlier in the day, Willis had been looking forward to seeing his home as he headed toward Culpeper. The brightly colored autumn leaves in the Virginia countryside made the trip even more enjoyable. Mosby's men enjoyed frequent furloughs as their rapid hit-and-run missions allowed them to return to their homes and farms often. But Willis' horse came up lame near Flint Hill, forcing him to stop at the local farrier's shop at Gaine's Crossroad. Suddenly, Willis and an unnamed companion were surrounded by troops of the 2nd West Virginia Cavalry. Taken prisoner, the two soon learned of their fate. One of them would be hanged. That order had come from General U.S. Grant as retribution for Federals that Mosby had killed: "an eye for an eye, a tooth for a tooth." Grant's order required that one Confederate be "hung without trial" for each Yankee killed by Mosby's men.

Speaking with the two young men separately, Colonel William H. Powell informed them they were to draw straws to determine which man would die. Powell also informed Willis that he could claim a Chaplain's exemption, if he so chose. Willis had not yet been ordained and knew he deserved no such consideration. He refused Powell's offer. The two prisoners were brought back together and ordered to draw straws. At first, providence seemed to have chosen Willis' unnamed companion to die. He burst into tears crying, "I have a wife and children. I am not a Christian and am afraid to die!"

Upon hearing those words, Willis spoke up: "I have no family, I am a Christian, and not afraid to die." Due to Willis' willingness to stand in his stead, the unconverted man was released. Within moments, after praying for his executioners, Albert Gallatin Willis was hanged and his limp body swung silently from a nearby poplar tree; the only sound heard being that of the hemp rope as it strained against the bark of the tree. After they were sure he was dead, the Federals rode off, leaving Willis' lifeless body hanging from the tree—a solemn warning to the rest of Mosby's men. As evening fell, three locals: William Bowling, Robert Deatherage, and John P. Rickets, cut down Willis' corpse and took it to the Deatherage home. There, his body was prepared and given a Christian burial. Today his remains rest inside a white picket fence in the graveyard of Flint Hill Baptist Church in Flint Hill, Va.

Many would say that Albert Gallatin Willis died in vain. But did he? Is it likely that the freed man ever forgot Willis' sacrifice and gift? Is it not likely that Willis' sacrificial death reminded his companion of another's sacrifice that offers us all another kind of freedom? God only knows what impact Willis' death had upon that unknown man, his children, his descendants, and the Federal officers who witnessed how well a real Christian dies.

Mostly forgotten by history, this young man's story of self-sacrifice is but one example of hundreds of similar stories that took place during the time of our nation's greatest struggle; stories of unbelievable courage and faith in God; stories that still inspire us; stories that remind us of man's cruelty—as well as his potential for goodness when empowered by the Gospel of Christ.

That, dear reader is what you will find within the pages you now hold in your hands. And author Michael Aubrecht's superb telling of these stories will cause you, too, to look upon these examples with admiration.

Richard G. Williams, Jr.
Huckleberry Hollow, Virginia

CATEGORIES

*courage. duty. faith. honor. mercy.*

# Daily Devotions

During the Shenandoah Campaign of 1862, Confederate General Thomas Jackson repeatedly proved himself to be a brilliant military strategist. Despite the strenuous demands of war, "Stonewall" still found time to hold Bible study and hymnal sessions with the officers of his brigade. Early morning devotions were a daily ritual in the Jackson household and the commander continued these sunrise prayer sessions even when on the march. Despite being an academic, he resisted the urge to glorify war, and routinely quoted battle accounts taken from the Bible in place of his own reports. Always eager to share his relationship with the Father, Jackson wrote letter after letter urging his countrymen (and women) to actively seek repentance. One letter, written to his sister, summarized his perception of the Christian faith:

*"You wish to know how to come to God; so as to have your sins forgiven, and to receive 'the inheritance which is incorruptible and undefiled, and that fadeth not away.' Now my dear sister the way is plain: the savior says in Mark XVI chapter, 16th verse 'He that believeth and is baptized shall be saved.' But you may ask what is it to believe? To explain this I will quote from an able theologian, and devoted servant of God. To believe in the sense in which the word is used here, 'is feeling and acting as if there were a God, a Heaven, a Hell; as if we were sinners and must die; as if we deserve eternal death, and were in danger of it. And in view of all, casting our eternal interests on the mercy of God in Christ Jesus. To do this is to be a Christian.'"*

# *courage*

Courage is the quality of mind and spirit that enables a person to face difficulty and danger bravely and fearlessly.

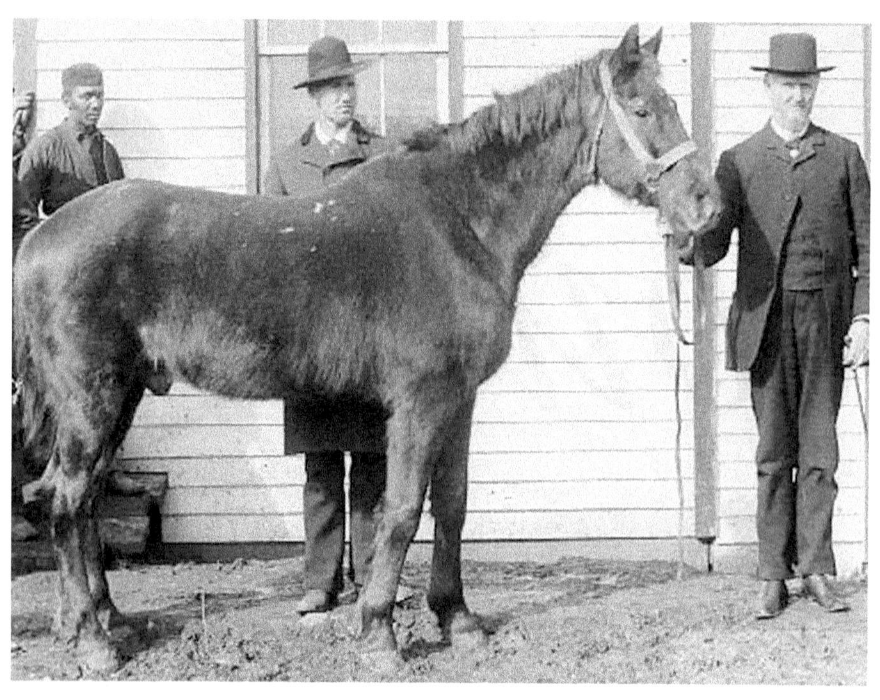

*Be strong and of a good courage, fear not, nor be afraid of them: for the LORD thy God, he it is that doth go with thee; he will not fail thee, nor forsake thee. (Deuteronomy 31:6)*

*His eyes were his chief beauty, being most intelligent and expressive and as soft as a gazelle's.* – Mary Anna Jackson in "The Life and Letters of Stonewall Jackson"

# His Master's Mount

The fulfillment of one's duty is the prime directive of every disciplined soldier, and executing orders under fire is crucial in achieving victory on the battlefield. Members of the armed forces are often called upon to follow their commanders blindly into desperate and dangerous situations without question—and without hesitation. Thus is the nature of man in war. Another loyal servant to the high command, whose contributions are overlooked, is the horse. Completely unaware of the politics, protocol and hypocrisy of war, this animal is more than just a mount. It is a faithful friend and follower who carries its commander into battle, possessed with the same courage as the humans around it. Perhaps one of the bravest of these commanders was Confederate General Thomas Jackson.

His most famous attribute was his unflinching presence and it won him the legendary nickname of "Stonewall" on the field at First Bull Run. A devout Presbyterian, Jackson believed that the time of his death had already been determined, thus no space on the battlefield was any more dangerous than the next. Like his master, Jackson's horse, Little Sorrel, ultimately became as beloved as its rider. No other horse, it seems, has been honored with such grace and dignity as this undersized steed. It is important to remember that every musket ball and exploding shell that Jackson faced, was also faced by his mount. Little Sorrel's service record, even for a horse, was extraordinary. Some of the redoubtable gelding's milestones included the First Battle of Manassas, the Seven Days Battle, the Battle of Fredericksburg and the tragic Battle of Chancellorsville.

As a testament to the animal's strength of will, Henry Kyd, Jackson's staff officer once remarked that he never observed a sign of either fear or fatigue from Little Sorrel. Following the death of his master, the beloved mount became a symbol of Southern pride and survived to a ripe old age. After he passed away in 1886, veterans had his hide mounted and preserved, where it remains on display in the Virginia Military Institute Museum.

*According to my earnest expectation and my hope, that in nothing I shall be ashamed, but that with all boldness, as always, so now also Christ shall be magnified in my body, whether it be by life, or by death. (Philippians 1:20)*

*Easy, but willing to die if God and my country think I have fulfilled my destiny and done my duty.* – General J.E.B. Stuart

# The Southern Knight

Confederate cavalry icon J.E.B. Stuart's first engagement with the Union Army took place on July 1, 1861, at the First Battle of Manassas (also known as the Battle of First Bull Run). Operating as a reconnaissance party, Stuart's men were successful in identifying the position of Major General R. Patterson, whose troops had crossed the Potomac River and advanced into Virginia. The early discovery of the invaders enabled Confederate General Joseph E. Johnston to deploy the future "Stonewall Brigade" to assist the cavalry north of Martinsburg. The result was a mêlée at Falling Waters, in which one Southern regiment, consisting of three hundred men and a single artillery piece, was able to suppress the attacking Federals.

During the skirmish, Stuart found himself in a dangerous situation that could have cost him his life. Fortunately, by the grace of God, he survived to tell the tale. While riding alone in advance of his troops, Stuart exited a densely-wooded area and unexpectedly found himself in the presence of a large body of Federal infantrymen. Riding toward them without hesitation, he directed some of the men, who probably mistook him for one of their own officers, to throw down their weapons. Apparently confused by the boldness of the charging officer, the men surprisingly obeyed. Stuart was able to secure their capture, aided by his arriving troopers, much to their shock and dismay. Consequently, the commander was credited with single-handedly capturing forty-nine members of the 15th Pennsylvania Volunteers.

Thus the legend of J.E.B. Stuart, the "Southern Knight," was born. And this would not be the last time he would manage to remain unscathed in the midst of such potential danger. Throughout the conflict, the cavalier would repeatedly put himself directly in harm's way while narrowly escaping death. Like his commander, "Stonewall" Jackson, Stuart firmly believed that God had already determined the time of his death. And, like Jackson, his religious convictions enabled him to rise to any challenge and inspire his troopers to hold fast, even in the face of total carnage. Often Stuart would acknowledge the protection of his Savior and consign his destiny to God's will.

*Watch ye, stand fast in the faith, quit you like men, be strong.*
*(1 Corinthians 16:13)*

*Oh, you of a younger generation, think of what it cost our forefathers to save our glorious inheritance of union and liberty! If you let it slip from your hands you will deserve to be branded as ungrateful cowards and undutiful sons. But, no! You will not fail to cherish the prize—it is too sacred a trust—too dearly purchased.* – Father William Corby from a book of his recollections entitled "Memoirs of Chaplain Life"

# Luck Of The Irish

According to Catholic doctrine, one of the most important duties a priest performs is administering the sacrament of Last Rites, which is a form of absolution given to a dying person. During wartime, men will obviously fall on the battlefield, mortally wounded and without the benefit of having a priest nearby. In order to compensate for this absence, Catholic chaplains would perform a universal form of this sacrament prior to the battle. This service was extremely important to brigades that were made up of immigrants such as the Irish and German contingencies. Perhaps the most courageous of these was the Union Army's "Irish Brigade," who deployed with the Reverend Father William Corby.

The Father extended general absolution to all soldiers, Catholic and non-Catholic alike. He was also known to administer Last Rites to those dying on the field, even while under fire. Prior to the conflict in the Wheatfield, on the second day of the Battle of Gettysburg, he offered general absolution to the "Irish Brigade." Despite the loss of 506 of their men during that day's battle, one soldier stated that, because of Father Corby, he felt as strong as a lion and had no fear, although his comrade was shot down beside him.

After the war, in 1865, Father Corby returned to Notre Dame where he was made vice president. Within a year, he was named president, and at the end of his term at Notre Dame in 1872, Father Corby was sent to Sacred Heart College. He returned to Notre Dame as president in 1877, where he became known as the "Second Founder of Notre Dame" for his successful efforts in rebuilding the school's campus following a devastating fire.

*Arise; for this matter belongeth unto thee: we also will be with thee: be of good courage, and do it. (Ezra 10:4)*

*And Thou knowest O' Lord, that when Thou didst decide that the Confederacy should not succeed, Thou hadst first to remove Thy servant, Stonewall Jackson.* – Father Hubert, of Hay's Brigade

# Thy Will Be Done

After a series of tremendous victories, the Confederacy appeared to be well on its way to declaring independence. However, the fortunes of war quickly turned in the Union's favor after the sudden and accidental death of the general they called "Stonewall." On May 2, 1863, during the Battle of Chancellorsville, Jackson's own men of the 18th North Carolina Infantry Regiment accidentally fired upon him, resulting in three wounds, and later, an amputated arm.

The accident occurred after the general and his staff trotted beyond their own picket lines in search of the retreating enemy's position. Jackson was quickly taken from the field on a stretcher and treated at a nearby hospital encampment at Wilderness Run. Initially, it seemed the wounded general would make a full recovery, but he later developed a fatal case of pneumonia.

Upon hearing his own prognosis, Jackson showed incredible courage and replied that he had always wanted to die on a Sunday. He said, "It will be infinite gain to be translated to Heaven." He then asked his wife to pray for him, but to always use the petition of "Thy will be done." In the end, he clearly accepted his fate as part of God's "Divine Plan," and resolved to spend his last hours before delirium set in, reading from the Holy Bible. The unwavering faith and spiritual strength that he maintained, even while on his deathbed, was a peaceful and tranquil gift amidst the madness of war.

Those present—his wife, doctor, preacher and comrades—were the most important people in Thomas Jackson's life. Their love for him and his Lord comforted them all. A few moments before he died, Jackson cried out, "Order A. P. Hill to prepare for action!" Then a smile spread over his face, and he whispered his last words saying, "Let us cross over the river and rest under the shade of the trees." It was a glorious finale to a glorious life.

*But Christ as a son over his own house; whose house are we, if we hold fast the confidence and the rejoicing of the hope firm unto the end.* (Hebrews 3:6)

*Never be haughty to the humble; never be humble to the haughty.*
– C.S.A. President Jefferson Davis

# Protestant President

Jefferson Davis was an American statesman who was appointed as the President of the Confederate States of America for its entire history (1861 to 1865) during the American Civil War. A man of humble origins, he began his formal education at a small, one-room, log cabin school in the back woods of Mississippi. Two years later, his family moved and he entered the Catholic school of Saint Thomas at St. Rose Priory, which was operated by the Dominican Order of Kentucky. At the time, Davis was the only Protestant student in the entire institution. His acceptance, as well as an introduction to a different denomination, made a lasting impression on the young man, who had been baptized as an Episcopalian.

Later, as a West Point graduate, Davis prided himself on the military skills he had gained in the Mexican-American War as a colonel in a volunteer regiment, and as U.S. Secretary of War under President Franklin Pierce. After rising to the highest chair in the newly established Confederate government, Davis made a concerted effort to bridge the social gaps between citizens of different faiths. During the nineteenth century, Catholics and Jews were often held in contempt and discriminated against by the country's Protestant majority. The Confederacy's pious President did not share this sentiment. Following his appointment to power, Davis set a major precedent by assembling the first administration in U.S. history that included Protestants, Catholics and Jews.

This courageous decision went against all previous political practices and ultimately sent shockwaves through the country's governing bodies, as not even his contemporary, Abraham Lincoln, had appointed anyone other than Protestants to a high office. In his article *Jefferson Davis, Religion and the Politics of Recognition,* D. Jason Berggren stated that, "Davis practiced the politics of recognition by appointing individuals identified with persecuted religious minorities. In this regard, contrary to conventional wisdom, Jefferson Davis was a remarkable president, a president ahead of his time."

*And he went up unto them into the ship; and the wind ceased: and they were sore amazed in themselves beyond measure, and wondered. (Mark 6:51)*

*"I've always thought the Yankees had something to do with it."*
– General George Pickett

# Pickett's Charge

On July 3rd, 1863, Confederate forces launched a desperate attack against the Union forces stationed on Cemetery Ridge, during the final day of the Battle of Gettysburg. After previous attacks on both Union flanks had failed the day and night before, the South's commanding general, Robert E. Lee, decided to strike the Union center on the third day. The bombardment that preceded the assault was the largest of the war. Starting at 1 p.m. and continuing almost two hours, hundreds of cannons from both sides fired along the lines. Rebel guns (numbering between 150 and 170) bellowed from a line more than two miles long. As a wave of smoke blanketed the field, approximately 12,500 courageous men, in nine infantry brigades, stepped forward out of the tree line and advanced over open fields for three quarters of a mile under heavy Federal artillery and rifle fire. Although some Confederates were able to breach the stone wall, they could not maintain their position and were repulsed with over 50 percent casualties.

In his book, *Intruder In The Dust*, William Faulkner wrote a tribute to the triumph and tragedy of the event: "For every Southern boy fourteen years old, not once but whenever he wants it, there is the instant when it's still not yet two o'clock on that July afternoon in 1863, the brigades are in position behind the rail fence, the guns are laid and ready in the woods and the furled flags are already loosened to break out and Pickett himself with his long oiled ringlets and his hat in one hand probably and his sword in the other looking up the hill waiting for Longstreet to give the word and it's all in the balance, it hasn't happened yet, it hasn't even begun yet, it not only hasn't begun yet but there is still time for it not to begin against that position and those circumstances which made more men than [General] Garnett and [General] Kemper and [General] Armistead look grave yet it's going to begin, we all know that, we have come too far with too much at stake and that moment doesn't need even a fourteen-year-old boy to think this time. Maybe this time with all this much to lose than all this much to gain: Pennsylvania, Maryland, the world, the golden dome of Washington itself to crown with desperate and unbelievable victory the desperate gamble, the cast made two years ago."

*Now when they saw the boldness of Peter and John, and perceived that they were unlearned and ignorant men, they marvelled; and they took knowledge of them, that they had been with Jesus.* (Acts 4:13)

*Major, I am not the same man you were with so long and knew so well. I hope I am a better man now than then. I have been and am trying to lead another kind of life.* – Nathan Bedford Forrest

# Saint And Sinner

Perhaps the most controversial of all participants in the Civil War, Confederate General Nathan Bedford Forrest has been both celebrated and condemned. Much of the argument surrounding the legacy of the general is due to his pre-war occupation as a successful slave-trader, as well as his post-war appointment as the first Grand Wizard of the Klu Klux Klan—although Forrest's incarnation was not the violent KKK that we know of today. In fact, the "Wizard of the Saddle" resigned his post after serving less than five years and officially disbanded the Klan's earliest charter in retaliation for the group's violent attacks on the local black citizens. Still, many have attempted to vilify the great Southern hero as being a lifelong racist. Forrest's abandonment of the Klan may not have reflected a shift in his critical attitude toward the Reconstruction policies of the Federal and Tennessee governments, but it did accompany a significant development in his views on race relations in his final years.

After coming to Christ and making an effort to follow his devout wife's example, Forrest came to see freed blacks as the key to economic recovery—and said so frequently in public comments, increasingly to the dismay of some ex-Confederates. Perhaps the best known instance of this new side of Forrest in his final years was his appearance at a convention in Memphis of a black organization, the "Independent Order of Pole-Bearers Association," on July 5, 1875. Forrest made a brief, but remarkable speech, which highlighted his emerging views on the race question. He said, "I came here with the jeers of some white people, who think that I am doing wrong. I believe I can exert some influence and do much to assist the people in strengthening fraternal relations and shall do all in my power to elevate every man to depress none. I came to meet you as friends and welcome you to the white people. I want you to come nearer to us. We have but one flag, one country; let us stand together. We may differ in color, but not sentiment. Many things have been said about me which are wrong and which white and black persons here, who stood by me through the war, can contradict. Go to work, be industrious, live honestly and act truly, and when you are oppressed, I'll come to your relief."

*And Joshua said unto them, Fear not, nor be dismayed, be strong and of good courage: for thus shall the LORD do to all your enemies against whom ye fight. (Joshua 10:25)*

*Stop, you little Yankee devil!*
– C.S.A. colonel at the Battle of Chickamauga

# Drummer Boy

One of the most remarkable stories to emerge from the Civil War is the legendary tale of a courageous youngster named John Clem. "Johnny," as he was referred to, ran away from home at age nine to become a Union Army drummer boy. He attempted to enlist in May of 1861 in the 3rd Ohio Volunteer Infantry, but was rejected because of his tender age and small size. He then tried to join the 22nd Michigan, which also refused him. Despite the rejection, Johnny tagged along and the 22nd eventually adopted him as the regiment's "official" mascot and drummer boy. Graciously, several of the unit's officers chipped in to pay him the regular soldier's wage of $13 a month and they allowed him to enlist two years later.

At the Battle of Shiloh, in April of 1862, Clem's drum was destroyed by an artillery round, making him a minor news item as "Johnny Shiloh: The Littlest Yankee." In September of 1863, at the terrible Battle of Chickamauga, he is said to have ridden an artillery caisson to the front and wielded a custom musket that was cut down to his size. In the course of a Union retreat, he shot a Confederate colonel who demanded his surrender. After the battle, the "Drummer Boy of Chickamauga" was promoted to a sergeant, becoming the youngest soldier ever to be a noncommissioned officer in the Federal Army. In October of 1863, Clem was captured in Georgia by the Confederate cavalry while standing duty as a train guard. He was exchanged a short time later, but the Confederate newspapers used his age to show "what sore straits the Yankees are driven, when they have to send their babies out to fight us."

Heralded as a national hero, Clem continued to enjoy celebrity-like status in the years following the war. He returned to his book studies and graduated from high school in 1870. After being rejected as a candidate for the United States Military Academy at West Point, former Union General and President Ulysses S. Grant appointed him as a second lieutenant in the 24th Infantry. Following his death in 1937, Clem was buried on the military's most hallowed grounds, Arlington National Cemetery.

# *duty*

Duty is what one is expected to do by moral obligation.
It is the fulfillment of a specific, and often personal, promise.

*Now the children of Israel after their number, to wit, the chief fathers and captains of thousands and hundreds, and their officers that served the king in any matter of the courses, which came in and went out month by month throughout all the months of the year, of every course were twenty and four thousand. (1 Chronicles 27:1)*

*Your note, requesting for publication, a copy of the sermon...is before me. In reply I would state, that if in your judgment its publication will in any way help us in the struggle in which we are now engaged, the manuscript is at your disposal.* – Rev. J. W. Tucker

# Providence In War

Throughout the course of the Civil War, many of the Confederacy's chaplains presented a myriad of empowering sermons to their flocks in the field. More than just invocations, these brilliant, impassioned speeches inspired the Southern soldiers to overcome many challenges that confronted them. Lacking the industrial resources or manpower of their enemies from the North, the rebel army repeatedly beat the odds in defeating much larger and better-equipped Federal troops. Many of these victories came out of seemingly hopeless situations, yet somehow the Confederates were able to persevere through sheer will power and mental strength. Much of their resolve came from the message of these sermons and the fervent belief that Almighty God had blessed their cause. One of these motivational homilies came courtesy of the Rev. J.W. Tucker of Fayetteville, North Carolina. On May 16th, 1862, the good Reverend addressed his congregation with a sermon that would later be published by the Presbyterian Church. In it he addressed the troops, calling them to stand firm in their duties:

"Soldiers of the South, be firm, be courageous, be brave; be faithful to your God, your country and yourselves and you shall be invincible. Never forget that the patriot, like the Christian, is immortal till his work is finished. You are fighting for every thing that is near and dear and sacred to you as men, as Christians and as patriots; for country, for home, for property, for the honor of mothers, daughters, wives, sisters and loved ones. Your cause is the cause of God, of Christ, of humanity. It is a conflict of truth with error—of the Bible with Northern infidelity—of a pure Christianity with Northern fanaticism—of liberty with despotism—of right with might. In such a cause victory is not with the greatest numbers, nor the heaviest artillery, but with the good, the pure, the true, the noble, the brave. We are proud of you and grateful to you for the victories of the past. We look to your valor and prowess, under the blessing of God, for the triumphs of the future..."

*Let us hear the conclusion of the whole matter:*
*Fear God, and keep his commandments: for this is the*
*whole duty of man. (Ecclesiastes 12:13)*

*In this short period of thirty-one years, four months and twelve days, he won a glorious and imperishable name and one that posterity will delight to cherish and honor.* – Captain R. E. Frayser, member of Stuart's staff

# Christian Cavalier

James Ewell Brown (J.E.B.) Stuart was born in Patrick County, Virginia, in 1833. His lineage was that of a Scotch Presbyterian, his forebears having immigrated to the Americas seeking refuge from religious persecution. Thanks to a distinguished ancestry, it's not surprising that Stuart men were widely known as gentlemen of great virtue. Both their Christian roots and their sincere appreciation for religious freedoms inspired them to give back to the community whenever possible. Their undying commitment to serve God provided a foundation of values and morality that benefited the family for generations to come.

After turning fourteen, Stuart enrolled in school at Wytheville. He was then accepted into Emory and Henry College in Washington County in 1848, named for Bishop John Emory of the Methodist Church and Patrick Henry, E.H.C. During his time there, Stuart participated in a revival of religion among the students. Although his mother was an active member of the Episcopal Church and his father was a Presbyterian, Stuart enthusiastically professed a conversion to the Methodist faith. Ten years later, in 1859, he returned to his mother's church and was confirmed as an Episcopalian by Bishop Hawks of St. Louis.

At the start of the Civil War, the pious cavalier went above and beyond the call of duty by graciously providing chaplains for all of his regiments and regularly encouraging group prayer sessions as well as religious meetings. The result of his efforts eventually led to the establishment of the Chaplain's Association, which held large gatherings encompassing the entire Confederate force in the winters of both 1863 and 1864.

*That I should be the minister of Jesus Christ to the Gentiles, ministering the gospel of God, that the offering up of the Gentiles might be acceptable, being sanctified by the Holy Ghost. (Romans 15:16)*

*It was a noble sight to see there those who led our armies to victory and upon whom the eyes of the nation are turned with admiration and gratitude, melted in tears at the story of the cross and the exhibition of the love of God to the repenting and return sinner.* – Thomas Jackson recalling the success of the Rev. Lacy's ministry

# The Good Shepherd

Despite the lack of readily available clergymen in the early Confederate States Army, several of the South's more pious commanders, including General Thomas "Stonewall" Jackson, appointed personal ministers to their staff and maintained daily prayer rituals whether in camp or on the march. One of the local Fredericksburg Presbyterian preachers, the Reverend Beverly Tucker Lacy, was appointed as the staff chaplain for Jackson and his Second Corps.

Answering the call of duty, the minister routinely led the worship services for the entire camp, which were often attended by General Lee and his staff. Reverend Lacy's energizing speeches quickly became a popular event for saved and unsaved soldiers alike who attended his sermons by the thousands.

It was Reverend Lacy who was also present with General Jackson after his tragic wounding at the Battle of Chancellorsville and it was he who took Jackson's amputated arm to his brother's farm in Ellwood Plantation for burial. After Jackson's death, the Reverend stayed on with the Second Corps as headquarters chaplain under Lieutenant General Richard Ewell. The tidal wave of questions that asked God's reasons for taking Jackson rolled over the "Stonewall Brigade," leaving a state of doubt and depression in its wake.

Reverend Lacy did his best to comfort the troops, believing that God intended to emphasize Jackson's Christian and military virtues by taking him at the height of his career. He agreed with his peers that God desired to teach the South to trust in no man, but in God alone. He also added that perhaps God was disciplining Southerners for their sins (including the sin of idolizing Jackson), but that the South would, in time, regain divine favor.

*And Paul, earnestly beholding the council, said, Men and brethren, I have lived in all good conscience before God until this day. (Acts 23:1)*

*Noble heart! Pure knight! Many are the tears which I have seen do honor to thy memory from those whose hearts were won by little acts of courtesy such as this.* – Major H.B. McClellan

# Rock Of Ages

On May 8, 1864, an invigorated Union Army left their camp at Spotsylvania Courthouse en route to Richmond. General Phil Sheridan stated with the utmost confidence that he could defeat all defending forces, including General J.E.B. Stuart and his Confederate cavalry. Stuart himself went on the offensive and rode south to prepare to engage the enemy at a strategically superior location known as Yellow Tavern. Sheridan's column reached the crossroads within an hour of the Confederates' arrival and proceeded to launch a major attack on the left.

As the Federals withdrew, Private John A. Huff of the 5th Michigan Cavalry hurriedly fired his pistol into a group of mounted troopers by the Telegraph Road. Instantly Stuart clutched his side. His head dipped and his plumed hat fell in the dust. Looking down at his bleeding abdomen, he calmly whispered, "I am shot."

As several of his troopers rushed to his aid, the wounded general scolded them, yelling, "Go back! Go back! Do your duty as I've done mine." Fleeing the ensuing battle, an ambulance managed to evacuate Stuart to the house of his brother-in-law on Grace Street in Richmond. After placing the commander in bed, the wound was inspected and judged mortal. Perhaps the calmest of all that were present, the horseman consigned himself to the inevitable and stated that he simply hoped he would live long enough to see his beloved wife and children.

With his worldly matters concluded, Stuart focused his remaining thoughts on the journey that lay ahead. He turned to the Reverend Peterkin of the Episcopal Church and asked him to sing his favorite hymn, commencing, "Rock of ages cleft for me, Let me hide myself in thee…" Then he joined the minister and his staff in prayer. At about 7:30 p.m. on May 12, he said his last words to the doctor, stating, "I am going fast now. I am resigned. God's will be done." He was 31 years old.

*And the captains over the hundreds did according to all things that Jehoiada the priest commanded: and they took every man his men that were to come in on the sabbath, with them that should go out on the sabbath, and came to Jehoiada the priest. (2 Kings 11:9)*

*There are things in the Old Book, which I may not be able to explain, but I fully accept it as the infallible Word of God and receive its teachings as inspired by the Holy Spirit.* – Robert E. Lee

# God And General

Like all soldiers answering the call of duty, officers in the Civil War suffered the same hardships and sacrifices as the men they commanded. Aside from the obvious lack of comforts, perhaps the most difficult burden endured was the absence of loved ones. After all, for every combatant deployed in the field, there were family and friends who were left behind. Adding to this heartache was the inability to be available when their spouses and children needed them most. Not even Robert E. Lee, the supreme commander of the Confederate Army, could escape this kind of personal tragedy. Like his subordinate, J.E.B. Stuart, General Lee lost a daughter while on campaign. The news of her passing was devastating and though he struggled with guilt, his military responsibilities prevented him from attending her funeral.

If not for Lee's unrelenting faith in the sovereign counsel of God, he may not have had the strength to carry on. Upon hearing of the death of his 23-year-old daughter, Annie, he determined that the painful event was part of God's Divine Plan and insisted that these words be carved on her tombstone: "Perfect and true are all His ways, whom Heaven adores and earth obeys." In his *Personal Reminiscences, Anecdotes and Letters of Gen. Robert E. Lee*, the Reverend J. William Jones recalled, "If I ever come in contact with a sincere, devout Christian, one who, seeing himself to be a sinner, trusted alone in the merits of Christ, who humbly tried to walk the path of duty, 'looking unto Jesus' as the author and finisher of his faith and whose piety constantly exhibited itself in his daily life, that man was General R. E. Lee."

Revered as one of the greatest military commanders in the history of warfare, General Lee also possessed a spiritual strength off the battlefield. He considered himself a sinner who had been saved, not by church attendance or by good works or by any other human endeavor, but solely by the grace of God and the blood of Christ. His duty was not only to the Confederate States of America, but also, more importantly, to the Lord above.

*And this is the charge of their burden, according to all their service in the tabernacle of the congregation; the boards of the tabernacle, and the bars thereof, and the pillars thereof, and sockets thereof. (Numbers 4:31)*

*It was my privilege to hear him pray several times in the army and if I ever heard a fervent effectual prayer, it was offered by this stern soldier.* – Rev. Dr. William S. White

# Pledge To Pray

After converting from a non-practicing Episcopalian to an eager Presbyterian, Thomas J. Jackson met the man who would eventually become his spiritual mentor, the Reverend Doctor William S. White, of the Lexington Presbyterian Church. White recognized Jackson's thirst for religion and provided him with a tremendous wealth of guidance and knowledge in the ways of practicing faith.

One Sunday during the sermon, the good Reverend Doctor suggested that every male member of the congregation should make an effort to lead his fellow worshippers in public prayer. Still relatively new to the church, Jackson was put off by this notion and did not feel he was either ready or worthy to fulfill such an important obligation.

Rev. Dr. White later recalled the ensuing conversation between Jackson and a church elder regarding his reluctance. He stated that the next day, a faithful elder of the church asked Major Jackson what he thought of the doctrine of the sermon and if he was not convinced that he ought to lead in public prayer. He replied, "I do not think it (is) my duty." Soon after, he was called on and made such a stammering effort that the pastor felt badly for him and Thomas was greatly mortified. Several subsequent efforts resulted in little improvement.

Despite this, Jackson vehemently pledged that he would fulfill this duty. "My comfort has nothing in the world to do with it, sir. You, as my pastor, think that it is my duty to lead in public prayer—I think so too—and by God's grace I mean to do it. I wish you would please be so good as to call on me more frequently." The Rev. Dr. White said that he saw from Jackson's reply and manner that he meant to succeed and that he gradually improved until he became one of the most gifted men in prayer in his church.

*So likewise ye, when ye shall have done all those things which are commanded you, say, We are unprofitable servants: we have done that which was our duty to do. (Luke 17:10)*

*Onward, Christian soldiers, marching as to war, With the cross of Jesus going on before.* – Sabine Baring-Gould hymn lyrics

# Christian Soldiers

The excerpt below is from a tract that was distributed to Confederate soldiers in camp and on the battlefield during the War for Southern Independence. It was entitled *The Christian Soldier, The True Hero:*

Soldier—A friend presents to you these little leaves. Now, while the peaceful Sabbath is wooing you to thought and contemplation, or while the soft twilight invites to quiet and repose, or while the faintly gilded East allows you a leisure hour before the arduous routine of the day; take them and bind them to your heart and emulate the picture therein portrayed. For what have you left your sunny home: For what do you uncomplainingly submit to the hardship of the camp? For what do you willingly expose your life on the dread day of battle? Do you simply seek the "bubble reputation of the cannon's mouth;" is your ear charmed by the hoarse din of war and the clang of arms; or, rather, does the pure flame of patriotism impel you to vindicate the cause of honor, virtue, liberty and the South? We will not insult your manhood by supposing that another or a baser motive than this has called you to the field.

This holy impulse can make you dare and do great things. It is heaven-born. It is the sublime gift of God. It is akin to the divine mind from which it springs; and he who is imbued with it recognizes the Almighty Hand in the direction of the affairs of nations and of peoples and to its sacred keeping entrusts his life and the fortunes of his country. With the glorious motto, 'God and my native land,' glowing and burning upon his heart, the soldier can seize his country's standard and, shouting to his followers to defend it, can, with steady hand, plant it upon the exposed parapet. He can unflinchingly bare his breast and, like the solid rock that Omnipotent Power alone can shake, confront the thousand deadly missiles of an embittered foe. He is prepared for the destiny that has been foreordained for him by a righteous God. When the loud clarion peal of 'charge' sounds in his expectant ear, he lifts his heart in an inaudible prayer to the Throne of Grace and with a whispered 'Thy will be done,' he rushes forward to the deadly struggle. *(*published sometime between 1862 and 1864)*

*Let the husband render unto the wife due benevolence: and likewise also the wife unto the husband. (1 Corinthians 7:3)*

*I believe he will be regarded not only as the most prominent figure of the Confederacy, but as the greatest American of the Nineteenth Century, whose statue is well worthy to stand beside that of Washington and whose memory is equally worthy to be enshrined in the hearts of all his countrymen.* – Lord Wolseley on R.E. Lee

# Christian Hero

Revered as a man of extraordinary character, General Robert E. Lee is still heralded as one of the greatest Christian soldiers in American history. In 1907, the Reverend Randolph H. McKim gave a sermon to the congregation at the Lee Memorial Church entitled *Lee, The Christian Hero.* The tribute recalled the virtue of one of Virginia's favorite sons and presented the foundation of faith, morality and Christian values that he exhibited while fulfilling his duties as a soldier, general, university president, husband and family man. He stated:

"The last ten years of his life are crowded with instances of sublime self-abnegation, patience, meekness, humility, resignation. Whence, we ask, had this man these things? Whence did he draw the inspiration for such grand moral victories? Came it from earth or from heaven? From man or from God? From philosophy or from religion? There can be but one answer. These traits of character—contempt of glory, meekness under injuries, forgiveness of enemies—are not inculcated by human philosophy, are not recognized in 'the code of honor among gentlemen,' are even repudiated as mean and unmanly by the world, while on the other hand they are inculcated by the religion of Jesus Christ (which Lee professed) and by that alone. …If you ask what it is in the personality of Lee which has conquered the hearts of the men who were his armed foes forty years ago, you will at once be told it is because men have recognized in him, from the beginning to the close of his career, the unfailing supremacy of duty as he understood it—because, in all the exigencies of his life, in every crisis of conduct, in his public and in his private relations, in the domestic circle as well as in the great stage of public affairs, he was himself the finest illustration of his own oft quoted saying, 'Duty is the grandest word in the English language.' Yes, through all his varied career, to the very close of his life, no one has ever been able to point to an act of his that was inconsistent with the supreme allegiance to duty…"

63
69

# *faith*

Faith is a belief that is not based on proof. It is confidence or trust in God and the doctrines or teachings of religion.

*Only fear the LORD, and serve him in truth with all your heart: for consider how great things he hath done for you.* (1 Samuel 12:24)

*This strength General Jackson eminently possessed. He walked in the fear of God, with a perfect heart, keeping all His commandments and ordinances, blameless. Never has it been my happiness to know one of greater purity of life, or more regular and devout habits of prayer.*
– Rev. R. L. Dabney, D.D., Theological Seminary, Va.

# The Bible Brigade

Throughout the course of history, the influence of the Bible has ended wars between empires and liberated nations. Therefore, it is no surprise that many of the world's greatest political leaders and military generals relied heavily on its passages for wisdom and truth. One of these generals was a devout and fervent student of the Word named Thomas Jackson. In addition to being among the greatest of all Confederate commanders, Jackson was also a Presbyterian deacon and one of the founding members of the Rockbridge Bible Society. As the chairman of the society's Board of Managers, he took on the responsibility of fundraising for the printing of Gospel literature.

Among Jackson's many favorite Bible verses was the Fifth Chapter of Second Corinthians, which was recorded as the last scripture that he shared with his wife before going off to serve his God and country. It states, "For we know that if the earthly house of this tabernacle were dissolved, we have a building of God, a house not made with hands, eternal in the heavens." Another cherished verse was Romans 8:28 which states, "And we know that all things work together for good to them that love God, to them who are the called according to [His] purpose."

When deployed in the field, Jackson maintained his obedient study schedule to the best of his ability. He remained a steadfast prayer warrior who began every day, at the first sign of dawn, strengthening his faith and pledging that Jesus Christ alone was his Savior and the only key to his salvation. It was this "daily bread" that spiritually nourished Jackson and ultimately gave him the courage and strength to become the legendary man we refer to as "Stonewall."

*By whom we have received grace and apostleship, for obedience to the faith among all nations, for his name. (Romans 1:5)*

*Let us trust in the good God, who has blessed us so much, that he will spare our child to us, but if it should please Him to take her from us let us bear it with Christian fortitude and resignation.*
– J.E.B. Stuart in a letter to his wife Flora Cooke

# A Child's Passing

In November of 1862, Confederate cavalry commander James Ewell Brown (J.E.B.) Stuart received distressing news from home regarding his darling daughter, Flora. Suffering from an illness, her health was rapidly deteriorating, much to the dismay of her parents. Unable to return home to be with his family, Stuart wrote letters to his wife every day expressing his concern, but also a resolution regarding the will of God.

One letter explained his inability to leave the field and encouraged his family to stay strong. He wrote, "I am entrusted with the conduct of affairs, the issue of which will affect you, her and the mothers and children of our whole country much more seriously than we can believe."

Unfortunately, Flora's condition worsened and she passed away a few days later. The loss of his little girl was heartbreaking, but Stuart maintained his faith in the Lord and looked to the day when they would be reunited in the Kingdom of Heaven. In a letter to his grieving wife he wrote, "When I remember her sweet voice, her gentle ways and affection for 'Papa' and then think that she is gone, my heart is ready to burst. I want to see you so much. I know she is better off, but it is a hard blow to us. I have been in battle every day since I heard of our darling's sickness, November 2nd. She died November 3rd and I heard of it on the 6th. I have been harassing and checking a heavy force, believed to be McClellan's. God has shielded me thus far from bodily harm, but I feel perfect resignation to go at his bidding and join my little Flora."

*And his name through faith in his name hath made this man strong, whom ye see and know: yea, the faith which is by him hath given him this perfect soundness in the presence of you all. (Acts 3:16)*

*That is an impressive testimony when you consider that during the war he was wounded 4 times, had 29 horses shot out from under him and killed 30 men in hand-to-hand combat. Yes the Lord had answered Mary's prayers and preserved him.* – Kenneth Studdard, Pleasant Grove Baptist Church, Summerville, Ga.

# The Wizard's Wife

Like many great men, Confederate General Nathan Bedford Forrest was blessed to be married to an even greater Christian woman. Her name was Mary Ann Montgomery. Spiritually, Mary was a great influence on her husband and he was ever remembered in her prayers. After the Civil War, Forrest recounted her influence to a friend saying, "Major, I am not the same man you were with so long and knew so well. I hope I am a better man now than then. I have been and am trying to lead another kind of life. Mary has been praying for me night and day for all these years and I feel now that through her prayers my life has been spared and I have passed safely through so many dangers."

After his wife convinced him to attend a sermon on a Sunday morning in 1875, Forrest listened as the pastor read from Matthew 7:24-27, which presents Christ's lesson on the difference between a "passive or non-believer" who builds his house upon the sand—and a "devout believer" who builds his house upon the rock. When the preacher finished, Forrest went forward, shook his hand and said in reference to the man who built his house on the sand: "I am that man."

The prayers of Mary Ann were answered. Nathan Bedford Forrest had come to Christ! He realized that all of his accomplishments, all of his victories and all of the religion in the world could not make him right with the Lord Almighty. Only Jesus Christ, the one foundation, could. From that day until his death in 1877, the "Wizard of the Saddle" lived each and every day for his Savior.

*All the paths of the LORD are mercy and truth unto such as keep his covenant and his testimonies. (Psalm 25:10)*

*Throughout his long military career, Oliver Howard gained victory by the force of his moral convictions, as often as by force of arms.*
– "The Civil War," a Ken Burns/PBS documentary

# Battlefield Believer

Much like his Confederate counterparts, Union General Oliver Otis Howard personified the nineteenth century Christian Soldier. Even in battle, Howard was as much a moral crusader as a warrior, insisting that his staff attend weekly prayer and temperance meetings.

In 1857, Howard was a full-time soldier who was deployed to Florida for the Seminole Wars. It was there that he experienced a conversion to evangelical Christianity and considered resigning from the army to become a minister. His religious proclivities would later earn him the nickname "the Christian general."

On the outbreak of the American Civil War, Howard, an opponent of slavery, resigned his regular army commission and became a colonel in the 3rd Maine Volunteers of the Union Army. After the war, he was appointed head of the Freedman's Bureau, which was designed to protect and assist the newly freed slaves. He even championed freedom and equality for former slaves in his private life by working to make his elite Washington, D.C. church racially integrated and by helping to found an all-black college, named Howard University in his honor. In addition, Howard was active in Indian engagements and subsequent relations in the West and is remembered as a man of his word and of strong moral convictions.

Much like his adversary Thomas "Stonewall" Jackson in the South, Oliver "O" Howard is to be credited for his evangelistic efforts on behalf of the North, in addition to his activism on behalf of all minorities living in the United States at the time. He was a man of God who ultimately became a man of the people—all people—regardless of the color of their skin.

*Verily, verily, I say unto you, He that believeth on me, the works that I do shall he do also; and greater works than these shall he do; because I go unto my Father. (John 14:12)*

*Since these numbers include only "conversions" and do not represent the number of soldiers actually swept up in the revivals—a yet more substantial figure—the impact of revivals during the Civil War surely was tremendous.* – Dr. Gardiner H. Shattuck, Jr.

# Confederate Prayer

Throughout the Civil War, a movement referred to as "The Great Revival" took place in the South. Beginning in the fall of 1863, this event was in full progress throughout the Army of Northern Virginia. Before the revival was interrupted by General U.S. Grant's attack in May 1864, approximately 7,000 soldiers, or ten percent of Robert E. Lee's force, were reportedly converted. By the war's conclusion, it is estimated that at least 100,000 Southern troops were introduced to the Biblical teachings of Jesus Christ. Often these "born-again" soldiers would carry prayer notes in their haversacks as a means of witnessing to others. An unknown author in the Confederate Army penned this petition, which has since become one of the most frequently quoted pieces from the war:

*I asked God for strength, that I might achieve,*
*I was made weak, that I might learn humbly to obey.*
*I asked God for health, that I might do greater things,*
*I was given infirmity, that I might do better things.*
*I asked for riches, that I might be happy,*
*I was given poverty, that I might be wise.*
*I asked for power, that I might have the praise of men,*
*I was given weakness, that I might feel the need of God.*
*I asked for all things, that I might enjoy life,*
*I was given life, that I might enjoy all things.*
*I got nothing that I asked for—but everything I had hoped for.*
*Almost despite myself, my unspoken prayers were answered.*
*I am among men, most richly blessed.*

*Now therefore fear the LORD, and serve him in sincerity and in truth: and put away the gods which your fathers served on the other side of the flood, and in Egypt; and serve ye the LORD. (Joshua 24:14)*

*Let us cross over the river and rest under the shade of the trees.* – Last words of Thomas J. Jackson

# Standing Like A Stonewall

Perhaps best known as "Stonewall," Confederate General Thomas Jackson earned his nickname at the First Battle of Manassas after refusing to withdraw his troops in the face of total carnage. After Brigadier General Barnard Bee informed him that his forces were being beaten back, Jackson replied, "Sir, we will give them the bayonet." Inspired by the bravery of his subordinate, General Bee immediately rallied the remnants of his brigade while shouting, "There is Jackson standing like a stone wall. Let us determine to die here and we will conquer."

A devout believer in predestination, Jackson insisted that God had already determined his time on earth and that no spot on the battlefield was safer than the other. Always eager to share his relationship with the Father, Jackson wrote letter after letter urging his countrymen (and women) to actively seek repentance.

One letter, written to his sister, summarized his faith. He wrote, "You wish to know how to come to God; so as to have your sins forgiven and to receive 'the inheritance which is incorruptible and undefiled and that fadeth not away.' Now my dear sister the way is plain: the Savior says in Mark XVI chapter, 16th verse 'He that believeth and is baptized shall be saved.' But you may ask what is it to believe?

To explain this I will quote from an able theologian and devoted servant of God. To believe in the sense in which the word is used here, is feeling and acting as if there were a God, a Heaven, a Hell; as if we were sinners and must die; as if we deserve eternal death and were in danger of it. And in view of all, casting our eternal interests on the mercy of God in Christ Jesus. To do this is to be a Christian."

*And now the LORD shew kindness and truth unto you: and I also will requite you this kindness, because ye have done this thing. (2 Samuel 2:6)*

*The path to glory cannot be followed with much baggage.* – Richard S. Ewell

# Conversion In The Camp

Not all gentlemen in the Army of Northern Virginia shared their commander "Stonewall" Jackson's passion for prayer. At times, their pious general's religious enthusiasm annoyed those who were agnostic, including members of his own staff. Several shared the notion early on, that General Jackson's dependence on prayer hindered his ability to make swift decisions when they were required.

One evening during a council of war, Jackson listened intently to various options presented by his subordinates. After they had concluded, he thanked them for their efforts, but added that he would present his own plans in the morning. Leaving him to ponder their strategies, Lieutenant General A.P. Hill said, "Well, I suppose Jackson wants time to pray over it."

Later that night, Hill's counterpart, General Richard S. Ewell, returned and observed his superior through the tent flap, on his knees praying intensely for guidance in the difficult movements that lay before them. Upon hearing the excitement in Jackson's voice and witnessing the sincerity in his heart, Ewell said, "If that is religion, I must have it." Up to that point, Ewell had maintained a bedrock faith in God, but organized religion no longer played an important role in his life. He did not own a Bible and his cynicism might be attributed to the horrors of war.

Despite this, he earned a reputation as an aggressive fighter and a leader who saw to the welfare of his men, an attribute that won him their love and devotion. He later attributed his own rediscovery of the Gospel and profession of faith to the influence and example of his commander. Following the untimely death of Jackson, Ewell assumed the post and services of his chaplain, the Reverend Beverly Tucker Lacy. Following the South's surrender, Ewell continued to practice his faith and eventually became a communicant at St. Peter's Episcopal Church in Columbia.

*But Jesus turned him about, and when he saw her, he said, Daughter, be of good comfort; thy faith hath made thee whole. And the woman was made whole from that hour. (Matthew 9:22)*

*No sight could be more touching than to stand near the chapel and see the wounded and the pale convalescents hobbling and creeping to the place of worship at the sound of the bell.* – Chaplain at Chimborazo Hospital in Richmond, Va.

# Baptism Under Fire

To this day, casualties from the Civil War (620,000+) still exceed our country's losses in all other military conflicts. From 1861 to 1865, both sides suffered tremendous fatalities and the subsequent damage to the country's infrastructure cost millions to rebuild. Perhaps if either army could have foreseen the tragedy that would befall them, a compromise may have been offered in place of cannon and musket fire.

One of the positive repercussions of the War Between the States was the number of soldiers that came to know Jesus Christ. According to some accounts, religion did not accompany many soldiers at the start of the war. The magazine *Christianity Today* recalled the trials and tribulations with living a Godly life while on campaign. It stated: "Day-to-day army life was so boring that men were often tempted to 'make some foolishness,' as one soldier typified it. Christians complained that no Sabbath was observed. General Robert McAllister, an officer who was working closely with the United States Christian Commission, complained that a 'tide of irreligion' had rolled over his army 'like a mighty wave.'"

Fortunately, as the war progressed, a movement referred to as "The Great Revival" took place in the South. Beginning in the fall of 1863, this event was in full progress throughout the Army of Northern Virginia. Approximately 7,000 rebel soldiers in Robert E. Lee's force were converted before the revival was interrupted by General U.S. Grant's attack in May of 1864. Dr. Gardiner H. Shattuck, Jr., author of *A Shield and Hiding Place: The Religious Life of the Civil War Armies*, reports that "The best estimates of conversions in the Union forces place the figure between 100,000 and 200,000 men—about 5-10 percent of all individuals engaged in the conflict. In the smaller Confederate armies, at least 100,000 were converted. Since these numbers include only 'conversions' and do not represent the number of soldiers actually swept up in the revivals—a yet more substantial figure—the impact of revivals during the Civil War surely was tremendous."

UNKNOWN
CONFEDERATE
SOLDIER

# *honor*

Honor is the virtue of honesty, fairness, or integrity in one's beliefs and actions. It is high public esteem, fame or glory.

*Honour thy father and thy mother, as the LORD thy God hath commanded thee; that thy days may be prolonged, and that it may go well with thee, in the land which the LORD thy God giveth thee. (Deuteronomy 5:16)*

*It is true that you have, to start with, good morals fortified by religion, a good temper and a good constitution, which if preserved will carry you through the trial safely. But the temptations of a camp to a young man of sanguine temperament, like yourself are not to be trifled with or despised.* – Excerpt of a letter from the Honorable Archibald Stuart (J.E.B.'s father)

# Parents And Principles

Following his graduation from the military academy at West Point, Second Lieutenant James Ewell Brown Stuart received a commission into the Mounted Rifles and orders for deployment to Texas. Rapidly adapting to his new duties and surroundings, Stuart immediately showed the potential to be a fine commanding officer.

In the spring of the following year, he was promptly promoted and transferred to the 1st U.S. Cavalry Regiment, located at Jefferson Barracks near St. Louis, Missouri, then assigned to Fort Leavenworth as the garrison's regimental quartermaster and commissary. The position offered great responsibility, but ultimately more marching than fighting.

It was during this period that Stuart became more intimate in his relationship with God. Often he would conduct a Bible study with his fellow Christian troopers and his dedication to the reading of the written Word grew more each day. Both the desolate location of his post and the lack of distractions may have played a big part in Stuart's salvation. His maturing demeanor and strict code of ethics also helped maintain an obedient lifestyle, free from disruption. As a young boy, he had pledged to his mother that he would maintain the family's honor and avoid the "ills of man," including alcohol, tobacco and gambling.

Amazingly, Stuart is said to have maintained this vow for the entire course of his life and only drank whiskey (a medicinal painkiller) on his last day at the insistence of his physician. This commitment and willpower signified his loyalty to the Lord and the spiritual strength that guided him.

*If any man serve me, let him follow me; and where I am, there shall also my servant be: if any man serve me, him will my Father honour. (John 12:26)*

*As it was, victory trembled in the balance for three days and the battle resulted in the infliction of as great an amount of injury as was received and in frustrating the Federal campaign for the season.* – Robert E. Lee discussing his defeat at Gettysburg in an 1868 interview

# Gamble At Gettysburg

Immediately following the loss of General Thomas "Stonewall" Jackson at the bittersweet Battle of Chancellorsville, the Army of Northern Virginia's commander Robert E. Lee became more reliant on his lower-ranking officers, including his favorite cavalry commander J.E.B. Stuart. After achieving victory after victory on their own ground, the Confederacy's supreme commander decided to take his army and the fight to the North.

In order to successfully maneuver on "foreign soil," the army became more dependent than ever on the scouting capabilities of its cavalry. In what could have been his finest hour, Stuart unexpectedly failed in the eyes of his peers. This letdown tarnished the legacy of an otherwise exceptional military career. It also resulted in a lesson in humility and grace.

During the first day of the Battle of Gettysburg, the Confederates accidentally engaged what they thought to be members of the local Adam's County militia. In reality, it was a force of Gen. John Buford's Union cavalry who had been riding ahead of the Federal infantry. At the time, General Stuart and his men were uncharacteristically absent, leaving the entire Southern forces without any reconnaissance capabilities. Later, Stuart attempted to explain his absence, and provided details of how he was forced to take a wider detour around the Union Army than he had originally planned. He closed his official report by stating, "Grateful to the Giver of all good for the attainment of such results with such small comparative losses, I have the honor to be, most respectfully, your obedient servant."

In a letter to his wife sent a few weeks later, he added his gratefulness to God. It read, "Upon the eve of another battle I write to say God has mercifully spared me through many dangers and bloody fields. My cavalry has nobly sustained its reputation and done better and harder fighting than it ever has since the war. Pray, without ceasing, that God will grant us the victory."

*Greet ye one another with a kiss of charity. Peace be with you all that are in Christ Jesus. Amen. (1 Peter 5:14)*

*The results of the last week must convince you of the hopelessness of further resistance on the part of the Army of Northern Virginia in this struggle. I feel that it is so and regard it as my duty to shift from myself the responsibility of any further effusion of blood by asking of you the surrender of that portion of the Confederate States army known as the Army of Northern Virginia.* – Dispatch sent from Grant to Lee

# The Peacemakers

On April 9, 1865, after four long years of fighting, General Robert E. Lee gracefully submitted the control of his Confederate forces to Union General Ulysses S. Grant at the village of Appomattox Court House in Virginia. By the end of May, all of the remaining Southern forces laid down their arms, bringing to conclusion one of the worst trials in American history and reuniting a country that had been divided in a great Civil War. Following several dispatches, both commanders agreed to meet at the house of Wilmer McLean.

Upon arriving first, General Lee was asked to wait in a large sitting room on the first floor of the residence. General Grant arrived shortly thereafter and entered the room alone while his staff respectfully waited on the front lawn. After apologizing for both his tardiness and ragged appearance, Grant began the conversation. The two veterans talked about their shared experiences in Mexico and moved on to a discussion of the terms of the surrender. At a little before 4 o'clock, General Lee shook hands with General Grant, bowed to the other officers and left the room. He then exited the house and signaled to his orderly to bring up his horse. As Lee mounted, Grant stepped down from the porch and, moving toward him, saluted him by raising his hat. All of the Union officers present followed him in this act of courtesy. Lee returned the gesture and rode off to break the sad news to the men whom he had so long commanded.

Years later, both generals met for the last time. Grant had entered politics and was elected the 18th president of the United States. Lee was the president of Washington University. Neither man wished to reminisce and avoided discussing the war. Their desire was to accept the results as God's will and move on together, in peace.

*To them who by patient continuance in well doing seek for glory and honour and immortality, eternal life: (Romans 2:7)*

*In Congress the talk, as I said, was of action, To crush out instanter the traitorous faction.* – John Reuben Thompson

# Paladin's Prose

In May of 1864, John Reuben Thompson composed a poetic tribute to a fallen hero entitled "Obsequies of Stuart." Having been born in Richmond, Virginia, in 1828, Thompson attended the University of Virginia, obtaining a law degree in 1845. His literary career took off when his father purchased for him a publication titled *The Southern Literary Messenger.* After the South's secession, Thompson served as assistant secretary of the Commonwealth of Virginia and edited both *The Richmond Record* and *The Southern Illustrated News.* He was also a frequent contributor to *The Index*, the Confederacy's British publication. His most prolific contribution however, was a post-mortem memorial to one of the South's favorite sons.

The poem was highly praised when it was published and beautifully honors the Confederacy's beloved James Ewell Brown Stuart. The black plume hat, yellow sash and charming demeanor helped turn Stuart into the dashing cavalier of legend. Still, as Thompson's prose recalls, there was plenty of substance beneath the style of the one they called "The Southern Knight."

*They well remembered how he loved to dash*
*Into the fight, festooned from summer bowers;*
*How like a fountain's spray his sabre's flash*
*Leaped from a mass of flowers.*
*And so we carried to his place of rest*
*All that of our great Paladin was mortal:*
*The cross and not the sabre, on his breast,*
*That opens the heavenly portal.*

*And thus our Stuart, at this moment, seems*
*To ride out of our dark and troubled story*
*Into the region of romance and dreams,*
*A realm of light and glory;*
*And sometimes, when the silver bugles blow,*
*That ghostly form, in battle reappearing,*
*Shall lead his horsemen headlong on the foe,*
*In victory careering!*

*Wherefore the LORD God of Israel saith, I said indeed that thy house, and the house of thy father, should walk before me for ever: but now the LORD saith, Be it far from me; for them that honour me I will honour, and they that despise me shall be lightly esteemed. (1 Samuel 2:30)*

*What he seemed, he was—a wholly human gentleman, the essential elements of whose positive character were two and only two, simplicity and spirituality.* – Douglas Southall Freeman on R.E. Lee

# Lee's Chapel

In 1867, construction began on the "Shrine of the South," otherwise known as Lee Chapel, on the grounds of Washington College in Lexington, Virginia. This sacred building was the fruition of a long-term goal of the university's president and former commander of the Confederate Army of Northern Virginia, General Robert E. Lee. After accepting an appointment to the school in 1865, Lee immediately recognized the benefit of having a sufficient house of worship on the grounds of the college.

In a letter sent to the school's Board of Trustees in 1866 he wrote, "A larger chapel is much needed. The room used is too small and badly adapted to the purpose. It is moreover required for additional lecture rooms, into which it could be conveniently converted." A newer and larger chapel that was capable of serving both the student body, as well as the surrounding community, quickly moved to the top of Lee's priorities. It was his first major undertaking as the president of Washington College and one that would serve the institution for many years to come.

One year later, in Lee's 1868 report, he wrote: "The completion of the new chapel, which has recently been dedicated to the service of Almighty God, is a pleasing as well as useful addition to the College buildings." Following the building's blessing, he routinely attended church there and was often visibly moved at the services. On one occasion, an associate approached the general, concerned with his emotional state. Upon inquiring as to what was bothering Lee he replied, "I was thinking of my responsibility to Almighty God for these hundreds of young men."

Although Lee Chapel still stands today, it was almost torn down in the 1920s after then President Dr. Henry Louis Smith stated that the structure was "unattractive" and not "architecturally compatible" with the surrounding campus. Thankfully, the United Daughters of the Confederacy mounted a public relations campaign that saved the building from demolition.

*And whether one member suffer, all the members suffer with it; or one member be honoured, all the members rejoice with it. (1 Corinthians 12:26)*

*The Confederate battle flag is associated typically with American values and American culture.* – John M. Coski in "The Confederate Battle Flag: America's Most Embattled Emblem"

# The Southern Cross

Perhaps one of the most recognizable symbols of the War Between the States is the Confederate battle flag, also known as the "Southern Cross." Unlike the national flag of the Confederate States of America (also known as the "Stars and Bars"), the Confederacy's answer to England's "Union Jack" continues to instigate both pride and contempt among heritage groups and civil rights organizations.

Originally, the national flag was intended to serve both government and military purposes. The "Stars and Bars," though popular with many members in the Confederate government, did not capture the imagination of the general public who seemed disappointed that their new nation was symbolized by such an unimaginative emblem. The design of the "Stars and Bars" was an unfortunate compromise, looking too much like the American flag for some Confederates and not enough like it to others. This also caused confusion on the battlefield early on, as troops had difficulty distinguishing between the Confederate and Union banners during several of the war's earliest engagements.

According to the Sons of the South, "The battle flag features the cross of St. Andrew (the apostle was martyred by being crucified on an X-shaped cross) and is commonly called the 'Southern Cross.' A large degree of the Southern population was of Scottish and Scotch-Irish ancestry and thus familiar with St. Andrew, the patron saint of Scotland. The stars represented the eleven states actually in the Confederacy, plus Kentucky and Missouri. This flag is the flap [banner] popularly associated with Robert E. Lee and is the flag under which he fought. The Army of Northern Virginia was the first to design a flag with the cross of St. Andrew and General P.G.T. Beauregard proposed adopting a customized version of it as the standard battle flag of the Confederate Army."

*Blessed be the LORD God of our fathers, which hath put such a thing as this in the king's heart, to beautify the house of the LORD which is in Jerusalem. (Ezra 7:27)*

*Next to the acknowledgment of his Maker was the thought of home and of the young mother with his child in her arms! The man of war was at the same time the most domestic of men. All his heart was centered in one spot.* – Mary Anna Morrison on her husband

# Widow's Weeds

During the summer of 1857, Thomas Jackson met a minister's beautiful young daughter named Mary Anna Morrison. She was a North Carolinian and like him, she lived for the glory of God. If anyone could have filled the void left by his first wife, Elinor Junkin's passing, it was Mary. And shortly after their introduction, the two fell in love. After a short courtship, they were married and settled into a modest house in preparation to start a family. Both became Sunday school teachers and were committed to the Word. Less than one year after their wedding, the Jackson's were blessed with a baby girl. They named her Mary Graham. Despite a safe delivery, the infant developed an illness and passed away a few weeks later.

At the time, it seemed incomprehensible that yet another childbirth catastrophe could occur in his lifetime. First, young Jackson's mother passed away giving birth to his stepbrother. Then his first love and unborn son failed to survive delivery. Now his newborn daughter had been taken just a few weeks into her precious life. Despite his grief, Jackson steadied his spirit. For most broken-hearted parents, the loss of a child is unbearable. For Thomas and Mary, it was a call to faith and an affirmation that God's will be done.

Both immediately turned to their Lord and the healing power of prayer. Later in their lives they were blessed with the birth of a daughter and named her Julia. Following her husband's premature death and burial in Lexington, Virginia, Mary returned to her native North Carolina to raise their daughter in peace. Faithful to the very end, she never remarried and wore the customary widow's weeds for the remainder of her life. After the untimely death of her daughter, who was only in her late-twenties, Mary took to the task of raising her two grandchildren and writing her memoirs as the wife of one of America's greatest generals. In 1898, she became the founder of the Stonewall Jackson Chapter of the United Daughters of the Confederacy in Charlotte, North Carolina, and participated as an honorary president before reuniting with her beloved Thomas and their daughter in 1915.

*It is a night to be much observed unto the LORD for bringing them out from the land of Egypt: this is that night of the LORD to be observed of all the children of Israel in their generations. (Exodus 12:42)*

*To your strength will be given the defense of the Confederate soldier's good name, the guardianship of his history, the emulation of his virtues, the perpetuation of those principles which he loved and which you love also and those ideals which made him glorious and which you also cherish.* – Lt. Gen. Stephen D. Lee, Confederate Veterans, 1906

# Sons Of The South

Shortly after General Robert E. Lee's surrender at Appomattox Courthouse in 1865, several organizations were founded to help with the preservation and presentation of the Confederacy's history and the legacy of her honored veterans. Two of the most active organizations are the "Sons of Confederate Veterans" and the "United Daughters of the Confederacy." For decades, both groups have established countless historical programs and events in an effort to share the stories of their ancestors with the public. Many of their statutes and charters revolve around the religious foundations of their forefathers. Boasting thousands of members all across the United States, the S.C.V. has ongoing programs at the local, state and national levels, which offer members a wide range of activities. Preservation work, marking and maintaining Confederate soldiers' graves, historical re-enactments, scholarly publications and regular meetings to discuss the military and political history of the War Between the States are only a few of the activities sponsored by local units, called camps. The S.C.V. official Web site outlines its philosophy for honoring their ancestry:

"The citizen-soldiers who fought for the Confederacy personified the best qualities of America. The preservation of liberty and freedom was the motivating factor in the South's decision to fight the Second American Revolution. The tenacity with which Confederate soldiers fought underscored their belief in the rights guaranteed by the Constitution. ...Today, the Sons of Confederate Veterans is preserving the history and legacy of these heroes, so future generations can understand the motives that animated the Southern Cause. The S.C.V. is the direct heir of the United Confederate Veterans and the oldest hereditary organization for male descendants of Confederate soldiers. Organized at Richmond in 1896, the S.C.V. continues to serve as a historical, non-political organization dedicated to insuring that a true history of the 1861-1865 period is preserved..."

# *mercy*

Mercy is a voluntary blessing regarded as the manifestation of compassion and favor. It is the act of showing kindness.

*Surely goodness and mercy shall follow me all the days of my life: and I will dwell in the house of the LORD for ever. (Psalm 23:6)*

*Weird, unearthly, terrible to hear and bear, the cries of the dying soldiers filling the air—lying crippled on a hillside so many miles from home—breaking the hearts of soldiers on both sides of the battlefield.*
– Confederate soldier at the stone wall, Fredericksburg, Va.

# Angel Of Marye's Heights

After crossing the Rappahannock River and taking possession of the small town of Fredericksburg in December of 1862, the Federal Army of the Potomac set its sights on taking the surrounding high ground where the Confederate Army of Northern Virginia had withdrawn. The most impenetrable of these positions was a long stone wall at the base of a sloping hill known as Marye's Heights. After several unsuccessful charges, the fighting ceased for the day, leaving the field littered with thousands of bloody Union bodies.

Throughout the night, screams and cries of the wounded penetrated the peaceful silence of the cease-fire. One soldier, Richard Rowland Kirkland, an infantry sergeant with the 2nd South Carolina Volunteers, struggled to rest amidst the horrid sounds of suffering that echoed across the battlefield.

By the next morning, he could take it no longer and requested permission to aid the enemy. With total disregard for his life, Kirkland grabbed several canteens and leaped over the fortification. Going back and forth over the wall for an hour and a half, Kirkland only returned to the safety of his own lines after he had done all he could do.

In 1965, a monument was sculpted by the artist Felix DeWeldon, and unveiled in front of the stone wall on the Fredericksburg Battlefield where Kirkland performed his humanitarian act. The inscription on the statue reads: "At the risk of his life, this American soldier of sublime compassion brought water to his wounded foes at Fredericksburg. The fighting men on both sides of the line called him the Angel of Marye's Heights."

*Or he that exhorteth, on exhortation: he that giveth, let him do it with simplicity; he that ruleth, with diligence; he that sheweth mercy, with cheerfulness. (Romans 12:8)*

*In their religious instruction he succeeded wonderfully. His discipline was systematic and firm, but very kind. ...His servants reverenced and loved him, as they would have done a brother or father. ...He was emphatically the black man's friend.* – Dr. William Spottswood White, Lexington Presbyterian Church

# Slave Sunday School

Regarded as one of the more pious heroes in American military history, Lieutenant General Thomas Jackson is still considered to be one of the most inspirational and eccentric of all the Confederacy's leaders. After returning to the United States following a tour of duty with the army in Mexico, Jackson joined the Presbyterian denomination. Later on, he became a deacon and generously donated one tenth of his earnings to the church. Eager to share his renewed faith with all people, Jackson was instrumental in the organization, in 1855, of Sunday school classes for blacks at the Presbyterian Church in Lexington, Virginia. Although he could not alter the social status of slaves, Jackson committed himself to Christian decency and pledged to "assist the souls of those held in bondage."

He continued his prayerful and financial support for the rest of his life and stayed in touch with the school even when on campaign during the Civil War. In a letter sent to his pastor he wrote, "In my tent last night, after a fatiguing day's service, I remembered that I failed to send a contribution for our colored Sunday school. Enclosed you will find a check for that object, which please acknowledge at your earliest convenience and oblige yours faithfully." Eventually the school congregation grew beyond the allotted facilities and ultimately blossomed into new churches for African-Americans.

In this regard, we can see how the evangelical white Christian slave owner had a positive influence on the spiritual education of those held in captivity. As a result, many ex-slaves became preachers themselves and were later responsible for some of the largest religious revivals that followed the South's surrender. Today, Jackson's ministry is looked upon with gratitude by the Christian ancestors of those who first attended the school.

*Let us therefore come boldly unto the throne of grace, that we may obtain mercy, and find grace to help in time of need.* (Hebrews 4:16)

*Long ago, when I first read about "Stonewall" Jackson and his playful time with little Janie Corbin, I wanted to paint it. I think the Christmas setting underscores the obvious love that Jackson showed for his little friend.* – Civil War artist Mort Künstler on his limited edition painting "Janie Corbin and Old Jack"

# Old Jack And Little Janie

In the winter of 1862-1863, General Thomas Jackson's troops made headquarters at Moss Neck Plantation, located on the banks of Virginia's Rappahannock River. Owned by Richard and Roberta Corbin, the estate provided a perfect location for stationing a weathered army in desperate need of rest and replenishment. Over the next few months Jackson developed an endearing friendship with the Corbin's five-year-old daughter, Janie. With Richard's absence, Thomas became an "adopted" father of sorts and Janie happily played the role of a *daughter who Jackson had yet to meet.

In March, General Robert E. Lee sent orders to initiate maneuvers for the upcoming spring campaign. Before departing, Thomas and his staff went to the Corbin house to thank the entire family for their service to the country. Upon their arrival, Janie's mother informed them that all of the children had come down with a fever. Jackson immediately offered the services of his personal surgeon, but was reassured by Mrs. Corbin, who cited her own doctor's prediction for a rapid recovery. After a short visit to the child's bedside, the general pushed on, well aware that another fight was on the horizon.

One day later, word reached camp that Janie had died from scarlet fever. The news hit Jackson hard, causing him to break down and weep. Although his tears may have caught some of his staff off guard, those who really knew their general understood the gentle spirit buried beneath the gritty warrior. Kneeling in prayer, Jackson may have found comfort in one of his favorite verses from Romans, 8:28, which states "And we know that in all things God works for the good of those who love him, who have been called according to his purpose."

**Julia Jackson pictured left with her mother*

*Blessed are the merciful: for they shall obtain mercy. (Matthew 5:7)*

*What could I do but go with them [Civil War soldiers], or work for them and my country? The patriot blood of my father was warm in my veins.* – Clara Barton

# Blood On The Battlefield

No inspirational study of the Civil War would be complete without recognizing the priceless contributions of Miss Clara Barton. Although she is remembered today as the founder of the American Red Cross, her only pre-war medical experience came when she nursed an invalid brother over a two-year period. In 1861 Barton was living alone in Washington, D.C. and working at the U.S. Patent Office. When her home state's 6th Massachusetts Regiment arrived in the city after the Baltimore Riots, she organized a relief program for the soldiers, beginning a lifetime of medical philanthropy. Upon learning that many of the wounded Federal troops from the First Battle of Manassas had suffered—not from want of attention, but from need of medical supplies—she advertised for donations in the Worcester, Massachusetts newspaper and volunteered to help with the organization and distribution of donated goods.

Due to her tremendous successes in petitioning for charity, U.S. Surgeon General William A. Hammond granted Barton a general pass to travel with army ambulances. Her orders were to accompany the caravans "for the purpose of distributing comforts for the sick and wounded and nursing them." For the next three years, Barton followed army operations throughout the Virginia Theater and in the Charleston, South Carolina area. Never far from the battlefield, she participated as both a hospital nurse and surgeon's assistant, following the Union's disastrous engagement at Fredericksburg and the Battle of the Wilderness. Her reputation for bravery and compassion attracted national notice and she came to be known as "The Angel of the Battlefield." At this time, she formed her only formal Civil War connection with any organization when she served as superintendent of nurses in Major General Benjamin F. Butler's command. By the war's end, Barton had performed most of the services that would be associated with the American Red Cross, which she founded in 1881.

*And there shall cleave nought of the cursed thing to thine hand: that the LORD may turn from the fierceness of his anger, and shew thee mercy, and have compassion upon thee, and multiply thee, as he hath sworn unto thy fathers. (Deuteronomy 13:17)*

*I said, "We have only won this day by hard fighting."*
*He [Jackson] was full of emotion when he turned around to me and said: "No, sir, we have won this day by the blessing of Almighty God."*
– Dr. Hunter H. McGuire

# Stonewall's Surgeon

Of all the regimental surgeons in the Confederate Army, none were revered as much as Hunter Holmes McGuire, M.D. Truly a talented individual, he was a brilliant surgeon, a highly gifted and competent doctor, a superb teacher, and a prolific writer and author. One Southern citizen remembered the physician as one who consulted with his patients "like a husband pondering the problems of the sick wife; the father looking down on the afflicted child." His contributions to Virginia, the Confederacy, the United States, and medicine as a whole, cannot be overlooked. At first he signed up to fight as a private in the Winchester Rifles, but McGuire was too valuable to serve as a foot soldier when the Confederacy needed trained doctors. Acting in the capacity of a surgeon, McGuire served under many different commanders. Among them were Thomas J. "Stonewall" Jackson, Richard Ewell and Jubal Early. It is, however, as Jackson's surgeon that Dr. McGuire is remembered. McGuire would later say, "The noblest heritage I shall hand down to my children is the fact that Stonewall Jackson condescended to hold me and treat me as his friend."

Following the end of the Civil War, McGuire published a series of papers reminiscing on his service to the Confederacy and especially his experiences as a trusted member of Jackson's staff. One of these essays recalled an event that personified the general's affection for men of the cloth. He wrote, "At one time just before the fight at Chancellorsville we were ordered to send to the rear all surplus baggage. All tents were discarded except those necessary for office duty. We were allowed at the headquarters only one tent and that to take care of the papers. A Catholic priest belonging to one of the Louisiana brigades sent up his resignation because he was not permitted to have a tent, which he thought necessary to the proper performance of his office. I said to General Jackson that I was very sorry to give up Father—that he was one of the most useful chaplains in the service. He replied: 'If that is the case he shall have a tent.' And so far as I know this Roman Catholic priest was the only man in the entire Confederate corps who had one."

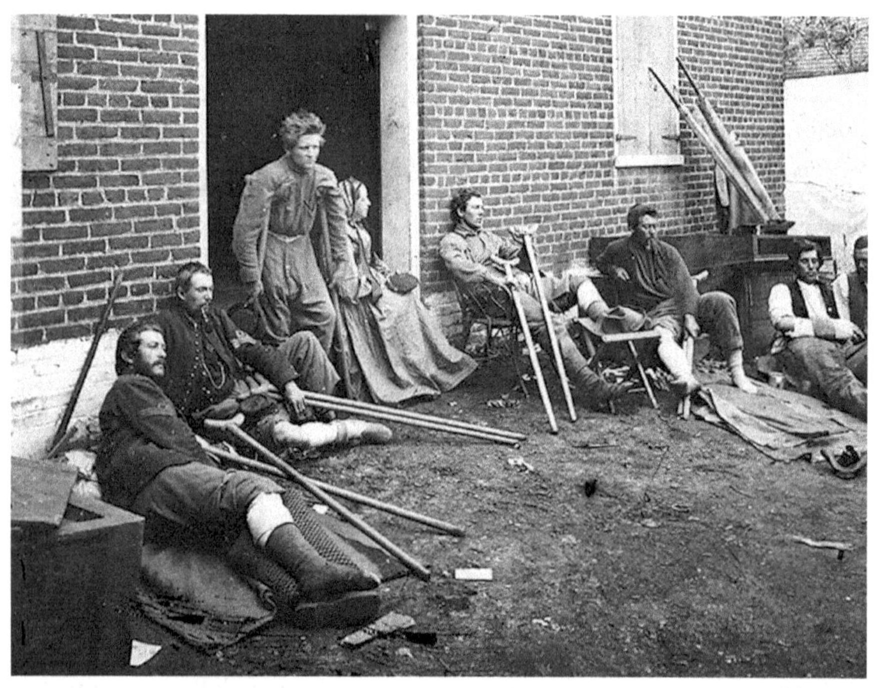

*Blessed be the LORD, because he hath heard the voice of my supplications. (Psalm 28:6)*

*I have never worked so hard in all my life and I would rather do that than anything else in the world.* – A weary nurses' attendant

# Mothers Of Mercy

According to the *Home of the American Civil War,* the increased ferocity of killing techniques that evolved during the conflict initiated a greater demand for volunteer nurses. It states, "For the unfortunate soldier, whether he came from the North or from the South, not only got into the army just when the killing power of weapons was being brought to a brand-new peak of efficiency; he enlisted in the closing years of an era when the science of medicine was woefully, incredibly imperfect, so that he got the worst of it in two ways. When he fought, he was likely to be hurt pretty badly; when he stayed in camp, he lived under conditions that were very likely to make him sick; and in either case he had almost no chance to get the kind of medical treatment which a generation or so later would be routine. Both the Federal and Confederate governments did their best to provide proper medical care for their soldiers, but even the best was not very good. This was nobody's fault. There simply was no such thing as good medical care in that age—at least as the modern era understands the expression."

Following an engagement, many of the nearby houses, barns, churches and stables were immediately commandeered for use as hospitals. Often, the local citizens of nearby towns would be inducted as nurses, surgical assistants and sometimes even as gravediggers. Approximately 2,000 women from the North and South served as volunteer nurses in military hospitals during the American Civil War. Miss Dorothea Dix and of course, Miss Clara Barton, were the leaders of a national effort to organize a nursing corps to care for the wounded and sick. Dix was already recognized for her work in improving the treatment received by the mentally ill when she began to recruit women to serve as nurses in the Army Medical Bureau.

A devoted nurse, she later praised her female colleagues stating, "They were gentlewomen in every sense of the word and though they might not have remembered that 'noblesse oblige' they felt and acted up to the motto in every act of their lives. My only wish was to live and die among them, growing each day better from contact with their gentle, kindly sympathies and heroic hearts."

*O' my God, incline thine ear, and hear; open thine eyes, and behold our desolations, and the city which is called by thy name: for we do not present our supplications before thee for our righteousnesses, but for thy great mercies. (Daniel 9:18)*

*Before she was searched, Emeline ate some incriminating information and tore up others, but much information was located hidden in her hoop skirt.* – John T. Marck in "Women As Spies"

# Southern Spy

In times of war, the act of espionage can become as valuable an asset to an army as its troops. History has recorded the legendary "cloak and dagger" lives of many spies who put themselves in harm's way in order to support their cause. During the Civil War, many women acted in this capacity, while gaining information and insights from (and for) their male counterparts. One of the most revered of these undercover agents was a woman named Emeline Pigott. On the farm where she lived ran a creek, and just on the opposite side from the creek bank camped the soldiers of the Confederate 26th North Carolina Division, whose duty was to defend Carolina's coastline. It was here that Emeline volunteered her services to the Confederate States of America, helping the sick and, at times, even nursing the wounded back to health in her home.

In addition, she collected mail from the Confederates, and gathered food, medical supplies and clothing, which she stashed in pre-designated hollow trees to be picked up by soldiers. Legend has it that she would conceal as much as thirty pounds of supplies while wearing an oversized hoop skirt. As the conflict continued, Emeline began to gather valuable intelligence from the Union cavalry scouts that periodically traveled through the area around her home. This information became a valuable asset to the rebel forces.

In 1862, the rebel troops of the 26th North Carolina departed for the battlefields of Virginia, but Pigott stayed behind and continued to spy on the occupying Federal forces. Three years later, she and her brother-in-law, Rufus Bell, were accused of espionage and arrested by the U.S. Army who prosecuted them as spies. Both were taken to the Federal prison in New Bern, where they were put on trial, summarily convicted and finally sentenced to death. Mercifully, a short time later, Pigott's sentence was mysteriously suspended and she was released on parole. Passing away in 1916, she never revealed the circumstances surrounding her miraculous release, but gave credit to the Lord for blessing both her and her captors with mercy.

*And when he heard that it was Jesus of Nazareth, he began to cry out, and say, Jesus, thou son of David, have mercy on me. (Mark 10:47)*

*So long as we shall deeply feel our dependence on God alone and put our trust in Him, He will favor us and our progress will be irresistible as the march of time. Faith is the principle of endeavor and endurance.*
– Rev. Joseph M. Atkinson

# Trust In Him

On September 18, 1862, the Reverend Joseph M. Atkinson addressed the congregation at the Presbyterian Church in Raleigh, North Carolina, with a brilliant sermon entitled "God, The Giver Of Victory And Peace." As with many invocations at the time, several of the church's elders later petitioned the minister to allow them to publish his speech in a tract format, so it could be printed and distributed to the Confederate troops in the field. In a letter, they passionately proclaimed the benefit of the piece stating, "...if sent to our soldiers in camp, as a tract, it would prove very acceptable to them and would tend to keep constantly before their minds the great truth—that to God alone belongs the glory!" Recognizing the higher purpose of his prose, Atkinson granted their petition and his words became one of the most popular tracts of the war. One section called his followers to put their trust in God alone and acknowledge His grace as their guiding light in this darkest of times. He wrote:

"In perfect consistency with this view, it may be affirmed as a uniform method of Divine Providence, springing, perhaps, from profound causes hidden in the nature of things and in the nature of man, that in all great Revolutionary movements, religious or political, the tendencies of the times should embody themselves in some one heroic individual whom all men are content to take as the type and representative of the whole period. ...When we come to our own day, may we not hope that Jackson, the Christian hero, the man of piety and prayer, with a fervency of spirit, like David's in the sanctuary and a martial ardour like David's in the field, has been graciously given us as the interpreter and impersonation of the Christian element and the Christian consciousness of this grand conflict. We cannot but regard it as a singular mercy of God, that the men for the most part who are the chief agents of Providence in conducting this Revolution, should be in personal piety, in such perfect correspondence with its religious character; and that the recognition of God in his incommunicable glory as Supreme Disposer of all events, should be so universal among our Rulers and people."

# Poet's Praise

Here is a case of a soldier I found among the crowded cots in the Patent-office. He likes to have some one to talk to, and we will listen to him. He got badly hit in his leg and side at Fredericksburgh that eventful Saturday, 13th of December. He lay the succeeding two days and nights helpless on the field, between the city and those grim terraces of batteries; his company and regiment had been compell'd to leave him to his fate. To make matters worse, it happen'd he lay with his head slightly down hill, and could not help himself. At the end of some fifty hours he was brought off, with other wounded, under a flag of truce. I asked him how the rebels treated him as he lay during those two days and nights within reach of them—whether they came to him—whether they abused him? He answers that several of the rebels, soldiers and others, came to him at one time and another. A couple of them, who were together, spoke roughly and sarcastically, but nothing worse. One middle-aged man, however, who seem'd to be moving around the field, among the dead and wounded, for benevolent purposes, came to him in a way he will never forget; treated our soldier kindly, bound up his wounds, cheer'd him, gave him a couple of biscuits and a drink of whiskey and water; asked him if he could eat some beef. This good secesh, however, did not change our soldier's position, for it might have caused the blood to burst from the wounds, clotted and stagnated. Our soldier is from Pennsylvania; has had a pretty severe time; the wounds proved to be bad ones. But he retains a good heart, and is at present on the gain. (It is not uncommon for the men to remain on the field this way, one, two, or even four or five days.)

– Walt Whitman, *1892 Prose Works*

# *essays of encouragement*

The life of a soldier during the Civil War was fraught with danger, death and despair. Faith was a key to survival.

IN MEMORIAM
RICHARD ROWLAND KIRKLAND
CO. G, 2ND SOUTH CAROLINA VOLUNTEERS
C. S. A.
AT THE RISK OF HIS LIFE, THIS AMERICAN
SOLDIER OF SUBLIME COMPASSION BROUGHT
WATER TO HIS WOUNDED FOES AT
FREDERICKSBURG. THE FIGHTING MEN ON
BOTH SIDES OF THE LINE CALLED HIM
"THE ANGEL OF MARYE'S HEIGHTS."

# The Southern Samaritan

Every Civil War writer has quoted either Union General William T. Sherman's statement of "War is all Hell," or the Confederacy's supreme commander, Robert E. Lee, when he said "It is well that war is so terrible—lest we should grow too fond of it." Both of these men were among the greatest generals ever to set foot on a battlefield, yet their obvious distaste for the very acts that made them legendary resonates from these lines. As a historian, one must always be careful not to "over-romanticize" war and to be constantly aware of the cold, sometimes harsh realities of the people and times that they portray. This is a dilemma that has plagued military critics for centuries, resulting in both revisionist and apologist histories being written again and again.

However, for every heartbreak in wartime there has also been heroism, and for every tragedy, there has also been triumph. This is what makes the history of warfare worthy of our attention and justifies the energy we spend to preserve its memory for future generations. It is the good stories, the ones that reflect life (not death), the ones founded on courage and mercy that demand our interest. This is the side of war that truly needs to be glorified.

One such incident is the story of Sergeant Richard Rowland Kirkland, otherwise known as "The Angel of Marye's Heights." Perhaps the most compassionate and heroic character of the entire Civil War, this lone Confederate soldier's conduct has become one of the most touching and inspirational subjects ever to come out of the War Between the States.

By the winter of 1862, Gen. Robert E. Lee's forces had claimed more decisive battlefield victories than their Northern counterparts due, in part, to the majority of engagements that took place on Southern soil. Throughout the first year of the war, the Confederates had managed to capitalize on a clear "home field advantage" by dictating both the time and place of most major engagements. As a result, the Confederate States of America appeared to be well on their way toward achieving independence.

One of the biggest and most "one-sided" victories took place during the Battle of Fredericksburg. Early in the morning on December 13, 1862, Union forces began a desperate and doomed assault on a fortified position, known today as the "stone wall at the sunken road."

After crossing the Rappahannock River and taking possession of Fredericksburg, the Federal Army of the Potomac set its sights on taking the surrounding area where the Army of Northern Virginia had withdrawn. Perhaps a little too confident after experiencing only minor skirmishes in the town, the Union commanders failed to realize the brilliant tactical deployments established by Lee's lieutenants. By intentionally leaving the town to the enemy, Confederate forces were able to fortify their positions in anticipation of the arrival of the Federals. The most impenetrable of these positions was a long stone wall at the base of a sloping hill known as Marye's Heights. Overlooking the field stood another "virtual" wall of Confederate artillery, cavalry and support troops that extended for miles in both directions. An attack would be a suicide mission.

In order to reach the enemy, Union soldiers had to ford a canal ditch and then cross a vast open field with little or no cover. As soon as they left the tree line, a massive artillery barrage, joined by almost uncountable rifle fire, rained down upon the advancing men. Those that were able to escape the cannon were slowed by a slope that led to a fortified stone wall lining a sunken road. Behind the wall, soldiers knelt two and three ranks deep, with the front line firing and the rest reloading musket after musket. The result was a continuous hail of fire that cut rows and rows of men down before they could even get into position.

Wave after wave of Union soldiers left the safety of the canal ditch and were slaughtered. The death toll was staggering. In just one hour the Federals suffered more than 3,000 dead. After fifteen unsuccessful charges, the fighting ceased for the night, leaving the field littered with thousands of bloody bodies. Around midnight, Federal troops ventured forth under cover of darkness to gather what wounded they could find, but many were too close to the Confederate line to retrieve. Throughout the night, screams and cries of the wounded penetrated the peaceful silence of the cease-fire.

A Confederate soldier stationed at the wall later stated that it was "weird, unearthly, terrible to hear and bear the cries of the dying soldiers filling the air —lying crippled on a hillside so many miles from home—breaking the hearts of soldiers on both sides of the battlefield."

One soldier, Richard Rowland Kirkland, an infantry sergeant in Company G with the 2nd South Carolina Volunteers, struggled to rest amidst the horrid sounds of suffering that echoed across the field. A combat veteran, he was accustomed to the dead and dying, having seen action at Manassas, Savage Station, Maryland Heights and Antietam. By the morning of the 14th, he could take it no longer and requested permission to aid the enemy.

Initially, his commanding officer was reluctant, as Kirkland would likely be shot dead by Union sharpshooters when he cleared the wall. He later granted the persistent soldier his request, but forbid him to carry a flag of truce. Determined to do the right thing and with total disregard for his own safety, Kirkland grabbed several canteens and leaped over the fortification. Instantly several shots rang out as the Union soldiers thought their wounded were under attack. Realizing the sincerity of Kirkland's effort, the Federal marksmen lowered the barrels of their rifles. Thus, the fatal shot never came and both sides looked on in amazement as the sergeant moved from one wounded man in blue to another. Going back and forth over the wall for an hour and a half, Kirkland only returned to the safety of his own lines after he had done all he could do.

A fellow soldier in Kirkland's company later recalled the incident in part of a short narrative entitled "The Confederate Veteran" that was published in 1903. He wrote, "The enemy saw him and supposing his purpose was to rob the dead and wounded, rained shot and shell upon the brave Samaritan. God took care of him. Soon he lifted the head of one of the wounded enemy, placed the canteen to his lips and cooled his burning thirst. His motivation was then seen and the fire silenced. Shout after shout went up from friend and foe alike in honor of this brave deed."

In the end, this soldier's action resulted in much more than a moment of mercy. It was a moment that stopped the entire Civil War and reminded those around him that, regardless of their circumstances, one should always strive to show compassion for his fellow man.

In 1965, a monument was sculpted by the famous artist Felix DeWeldon and unveiled in front of the stone wall on the Fredericksburg battlefield where Kirkland performed his humanitarian act. The inscription on the statue reads: "At the risk of his life, this American soldier of sublime compassion brought water to his wounded foes at Fredericksburg. The fighting men on both sides of the line called him the Angel of Marye's Heights."

It should be added that Sergeant Kirkland was not the only well remembered 'Good Samaritan' at Fredericksburg. Another 'angel' was administering aid on the other side of the field. As with all of the churches in town, the Union Army commandeered the Presbyterian's house of worship to use as a field hospital. The official reports following the Battle of Fredericksburg state that the Union forces suffered approximately 12,653 casualties. The Confederate losses were much less, but still considerable. Many of the wounded on both sides would die, not from their battlefield wounds, but from the disease and infections that would strike them after medical care and occasional amputations were performed. The conditions at these makeshift medical sites were far too often deplorable.

One woman who was determined to improve the health care of wounded soldiers everywhere was Miss Clara Barton, founder of the American Red Cross and celebrated Civil War humanitarian. Following the engagement, Barton crossed the river on the same pontoon bridges the Federals had used. She wrote of the horrors that greeted her on the other side stating, "I had crossed over into that city of death, its roofs riddled by shells, its very church a crowded hospital, every street a battle line, every hill a rampart."

According to her own accounts, she rendered aid to the sick and dying in both the Episcopal and Presbyterian sanctuaries. Barton also wrote of being called from church to church, even stopping to administer aid to a severely wounded infantryman who turned out to be the sexton of her own childhood church in Worcester, Massachusetts. She later returned across the river to the Lacy house at Chatham Manor, where she estimated there to be no less than 1,200 wounded men crowded into the twelve rooms of the mansion. Like her comrades in blue, Barton returned later in the war to the same town and churches to nurse troops felled in the bloody battles of the Wilderness and Spotsylvania Court House campaigns. The traumatic events of these wartime trials remained ingrained in her memory and a biographer later stated, "The memories of Fredericksburg remained with her, distinct and terrible, to the day of her death." As a testament to the goodwill and charity of Clara Barton, a bronze plaque was dedicated in the yard of the Presbyterian Church on September 25, 1962. It reads:

*In Memory of*

*1862-1962*
*CLARA BARTON*

*Founder of the American Red Cross, a devoted*
*Nurse and tireless organizer who knew no enemy*
*but the unfeeling heart. We walk the ways she took*
*in easing the suffering at the Battle of Fredericksburg,*
*when the churches became military hospitals.*

*Erected by*
*Civil War Centennial Committee of Fredericksburg*

EPILOGUE:

*"In September of 1863, [Sergeant Richard Rowland] Kirkland would find himself fighting in the western theater as a detachment from Lieutenant General [James] Longstreet's Corps moved west to support Confederate General Braxton Bragg's efforts to stop Union Major General William Starke Rosecrans and the Army of the Cumberland. They would do just that during the Battle of Chickamauga, which would produce both a Southern victory and 34,600 casualties. Sadly, the valiant sergeant ranked among those killed during this colossal battle. Mortally wounded in a failed charge, Kirkland exhorted his comrades to, 'Save yourselves' adding 'Tell Pa, I died right.'"*

– The American Civil War, "Angel of Marye's Heights"

JACKSON
ON THE FIELD
DEC. 12-13. 1862.

# Paternal Promise

One of the least known, yet most charming stories in the legendary life of Confederate General Thomas Jackson is that of "Old Jack" and little Janie Corbin. In the winter of 1862-1863, "Stonewall's" troops made headquarters at Moss Neck Plantation, located on the banks of Virginia's Rappahannock River. Owned and operated by Richard and Roberta Corbin, the estate provided a perfect location for stationing a weathered army in desperate need of rest and replenishment.

At the start of the war, Mr. Corbin departed to serve in the Confederate Army, while his wife stepped in to take over the day-to-day duties of running the plantation. A true Southern belle, Mrs. Corbin welcomed General Jackson's troops with open arms and allowed them full use of her grounds and facilities. As hostesses, Mrs. Corbin and her daughters entertained the officers with piano recitals or hymnal sessions. Home-cooked meals were also prepared for the senior staff. Jackson could often be found drinking lemonade on the front porch of the big house and it was during these regular visits that he developed an endearing friendship with the Corbin's five-year-old daughter, Janie.

Each day, Janie would visit the general's office, interrupting his daily review of battle accounts with his staff. Most times, Jackson would take advantage of the opportunity to relinquish his paperwork duties in favor of playing with his newest friend. On one occasion, Janie snatched the general's kepi hat and proceeded to march around the room, mocking his orders. Smiles immediately spread across the faces of Jackson and his aides and they laughed uncontrollably at the "littlest general" whose entire head was engulfed by a mass of floppy gray fabric and a wide black brim.

Innocence like Janie's was rare in war times and her wonderful gift of laughter lifted the morale of all that met her. Above all others though, it was her relationship with the general that quickly blossomed, nurtured by the fact that they temporarily filled a void in each other's life. With Mr. Corbin's absence, Jackson became an "adopted" father of sorts and Janie happily played the role of a daughter who he had yet to meet.

Thomas' love for her was genuine and Janie brought out a side of the general that none of his troops had seen. Some days they would race around the campsites, playing hide-and-seek. Other times Jackson would pretend he was a pony, carrying her high on his shoulders while trotting about. One of his aides later stated that it was truly an amazing site to witness the fierce commander who preached of swift and total destruction, acting like a father.

In March, General Lee sent orders to Jackson's troops to initiate maneuvers for the upcoming spring campaign. After carefully striking their camp, with the utmost respect for the Moss Neck grounds, the "Stonewall Brigade" prepared to move out. Before leaving, Jackson and his staff went to the Corbin's main house to thank the entire family for their service to the Confederacy. The general also wanted to have a few moments alone to give a proper goodbye to his dear little girl. Unfortunately upon their arrival, Janie's mother informed them that all of the children had developed a fever.

Visibly concerned, the general immediately offered the services of his personal surgeon, but was reassured by Mrs. Corbin, who cited her own doctor's prediction for a rapid recovery. After a short visit to the child's bedside, Jackson pushed on, aware that another fight was on the horizon. One day later, word reached the camp that Janie's condition had been hopeless and that she died from scarlet fever.

The news hit Jackson hard, causing him to break down and weep inconsolably for the loss of his friend. Although his tears may have caught some of his staff off guard, those who really knew their general understood the gentle spirit buried beneath the warrior. He would continue to mourn for some time, which prompted his aides to arrange a well-deserved surprise.

"Stonewall's" spirits improved one month later when his prayers were finally answered. Tears of sorrow quickly turned to tears of joy, as his wife and five-month-old baby girl were able to spend nine delightful days with him in Fredericksburg, Virginia. During that time, his daughter was baptized at the local Presbyterian Church and both parents proudly gloated over their little bundle of joy.

Unfortunately, his family's earthly relationship lasted but another month and this time it was Jackson himself who was taken away. After being severely wounded at the Battle of Chancellorsville, he later succumbed to a deadly case of pneumonia.

Perhaps "Old Jack" was welcomed at the Heavenly Gates by a little girl named Janie, who was waiting to play another game of hide-and-seek with the "gentle general." I can almost hear them now, laughing and running amidst the clouds, comforting one another until the day they were reunited with their own families.

# The Bible Brigade

People often ask themselves, "Why should I join a Bible study?" Or, "What can I *really* get from studying the Good Book in a small group?" The answer is simply another question. Why not? It is the best-selling book of all time and among our most valued of all earthly possessions. Its pages consist of sixty-six different books that contain the sacred origins of Judaism and Christianity. It is the (Holy) Bible and derives its title from the English form of the Greek name "Biblia," meaning "books," the name which, in the fifth century, began to be given to the entire collection of sacred books known as the "Library of Divine Revelation."

Sometimes it can really help to see an example of how studying God's Word can really empower us and make a difference in our lives. One story, in particular, reminds us of the real courage and conviction that can be gained by studying the holy scriptures.

Throughout the course of history, the influence of the Bible has ended wars between empires and liberated nations. Therefore, it is no surprise that many of the world's greatest political leaders and military generals relied heavily on its passages for wisdom and truth. One of these generals was a devout and fervent student of the Word named Thomas Jackson. Although his claim to fame had been primarily his service on the battlefield, it was the Christian man and not the soldier, who set a lasting example for Bible students today.

In addition to being among the greatest of all Confederate commanders, Jackson was also a Presbyterian deacon and one of the founding members of the Rockbridge Bible Society. As the chairman of the society's Board of Managers, he took on the responsibility of fundraising for the printing of Gospel literature. A serious student of the Word, Jackson was a perfect man for the job and dedicated himself to providing religious literature to spread the message of the Gospel of Jesus Christ to free Southern citizens as well as those held in bondage.

According to General Jackson's chief-of-staff, a preacher named Dr. R.L. Dabney, the daily ritual of intensive Bible study, as practiced in the Jackson household, was a mainstay. He wrote that Jackson always rose at dawn, had private devotions, family prayers, and then spent time in the study of scripture on and off throughout the day.

Among Jackson's many favorite Bible verses was the Fifth Chapter of Second Corinthians, which was recorded as the last scripture that he shared with his wife before going off to serve his God and country. It states, "For we know that if the earthly house of this tabernacle were dissolved, we have a building of God, a house not made with hands, eternal in the heavens." Another cherished verse, quoted in the work *The Consummate Prayer Warrior Christ in the Camp; or Religion in Lee's Army* (1888) by the Reverend J. Wm. Jones, D.D., was Romans 8:28 which states, "And we know that all things work together for good to them that love God, to them who are the called according to [His] purpose."

When deployed in the field, Jackson maintained his obedient study schedule to the best of his ability. As a steadfast prayer warrior, he began each day at dawn, strengthening his faith and pledging that Jesus Christ alone was his Savior and the only key to his salvation. It was this "daily bread" that spiritually nourished Jackson and ultimately gave him the courage and strength to become the legendary man we refer to as "Stonewall."

Wherever "Stonewall" went while on campaign, he always took his prayer book and prayer table, along with a bell for summoning his troops to worship services. Regular devotions and study times were also adhered to at all costs. At every encampment under his command, Jackson ordered a special tent to be erected as a field chapel, and at the frequent religious services that he held there, the general often acted as an usher for his own men and subordinates.

As both a deacon and Sunday school teacher at his Presbyterian Church back home in Lexington, Virginia, Jackson had gone through a spiritual transformation. It took him from a shy believer with little self-confidence and a fear of public speaking, to a fervent prayer warrior, whose passion for the power of God's Holy Word became an infectious motivator throughout the ranks of the Army of Northern Virginia. Once a quiet man, Thomas Jackson grew to become a seasoned speaker, capable of giving fiery speeches to thousands of men before each battle. Ultimately, his words became a weapon of their own, inspiring his men to overcome all odds in the name of their general, their God, and their beloved Confederate States of America.

Not all Southern gentleman shared Jackson's passion for prayer. At times, his religious enthusiasm annoyed those who were agnostic, including members of his own staff. Several shared the notion early on that Jackson's dependence on prayer hindered his ability to make swift decisions. One evening during a council of war, the general listened intently to various options presented by his subordinates. After the staff meeting concluded, he thanked them for their efforts, but added that he would present his own plan in the morning. Leaving him to ponder their strategies, Lt. General A.P. Hill said, "Well, I suppose Jackson wants time to pray over it."

Later that night, Hill's counterpart, General Richard S. Ewell, returned and observed his superior through the tent flap, on his knees praying intensely for guidance regarding the difficult movements that lay before him and his troops. Upon hearing the excitement in Jackson's voice and witnessing the sincerity in his heart, Ewell said, "If that is religion, I must have it." He later attributed his profession of faith to Jackson's influence and example. Following the untimely death of his mentor, Ewell assumed the post and services of his chaplain, the Reverend Beverly Tucker Lacy. Following the South's surrender, he continued to practice his faith and became a communicant at St. Peter's Episcopal Church in Columbia.

Determined to spread the Good News of the Gospel, Jackson's evangelism off the battlefield remained a top priority with him. Whenever his military services were not required, the general spent all of his mental energy witnessing to others in the name of the Lord. As the "Stonewall Brigade" continued to fight with honor, word of their general's religious zeal spread throughout the South.

A writer from the *Richmond Whig* described one of Jackson's speeches following the Battle of McDowell:

"General Jackson addressed his troops in a few terse and pointed remarks, thanking them for the courage, endurance and soldierly conduct displayed at the battle of McDowell on the 8th inst. [of this month], and closed by appointing 10 o'clock of that day as an occasion of prayer and thanksgiving throughout the army for the victory which followed that bloody engagement. There, in the beautiful little valley of the South Branch, with the blue and towering mountains covered with the verdure of spring, the green sward smiling a welcome to the season of flowers, and the bright sun, unclouded, lending a genial, refreshing warmth, that army, equipped for the stern conflict of war, bent in humble praise and thanksgiving to the God of Battles for the success vouchsafed to our arms in the recent sanguinary encounter of the two armies. While this solemn ceremony was progressing in every regiment, the minds of the soldiery drawn off from the bayonet and sabre, the enemy's artillery was occasionally belching forth its leaden death; yet all unmoved stood that worshipping army, acknowledging the supremacy of the will of Him who controls the destinies of men and nations, and chooses the weaker things of earth to confound the mighty."

Regardless of his unquestionable dedication to duty, one aspect of military service did not set well with Jackson. Throughout his religious renewal, "Stonewall" had strictly observed the Sabbath, refusing to take part in any work-related activities on Sundays. In war however, calendars are rendered meaningless and Jackson was often called upon to fulfill his military obligation in place of worship. As a result, many prayer vigils were held before and after battles in place of Sunday service. Whenever possible though, a strict schedule of morning and evening worship on the Sabbath, as well as Wednesday prayer meetings was faithfully maintained.

Protecting the sanctity of religious practices did not end with Jackson. The entire Presbyterian denomination, as well as their contemporaries, were extremely concerned about the repercussions of the wartime climate. First and foremost was the inevitable splitting of the denominations following the South's secession. And although there appeared to be no immediate hostilities harbored by Christian leaders on either side, the fact remained that the political split in the country—also split the church. This had a profound effect on virtually every aspect of their operations.

For example, up until the outbreak of the Civil War, the American Bible Society, based in New York, handled the production and distribution of most Protestant-based materials including Bibles and tracts. After the conflict began, an entirely new system had to be formed in order to meet the needs of the Southern congregations. Many of these dilemmas were addressed in the minutes of the Presbyterian Church's General Assembly. One major point addressed the need to establish a new chapter of the Bible Society to shoulder the task of producing and distributing materials in the Confederate states.

Another concern pertained to the issue of camp worship and the negative effects of military operations on the Sabbath. A letter was therefore drafted and forwarded to Confederate President Jefferson Davis. It stated:

"To the President of the Confederate States of America: Sir: The General Assembly of the Presbyterian Church in the Confederate States of America venture to address your Excellency in reference to the desecration of the Sabbath in our armies. In common with very many of our fellow-citizens, we have been deeply pained at the prevailing disregard of an institution which lies at the foundation, not only of Christianity, but of morality as well. The God who ordained the Sabbath is that God to whom we are accustomed to appeal for the justice of our cause—upon whom we are calling for that help which alone can avail to bring our country successfully and triumphantly through the present great struggle. How can we hope for God's blessing, or consistently ask it, when we are deliberately and habitually setting aside, and treating with contempt that which He has enjoined upon us to remember and keep holy. Surely never could circumstances more imperiously call upon us, as a people, to put away every thing which might be displeasing to that Great Being on whose favor we are so utterly dependent; and do not our soldiers and officers eminently require the salutary influence of the Sabbath amid the manifold temptations of the camp, and the fierce perils of the battle-field?

The Assembly have learned with regret that it is not uncommon for the military arrangements of the Sabbath to be of such a nature as seriously to interfere with the observance of public worship. The General Assembly would, therefore, respectfully request your Excellency to use your influence and authority as Commander-in-Chief of the Army, to do away with dress parades, inspections, reviewals, or unnecessary movements of troops on the Sabbath, and also to see that the officers shall not interfere with the observance of religious services, but on the contrary, afford all proper facilities for the same.

The uniform interest manifested by your Excellency in all that pertains to Christianity, leads us to hope that a matter of such moment will secure the attention it merits. Let us remember that "righteousness exalteth a nation," and that God has declared that they that honor Him will be honored, whilst they that despise Him shall be lightly esteemed. With earnest prayer to God that he will grant you, dear sir, wisdom and grace for your exalted and responsible station in these dark and troublous times, and with great respect, We are, &c."

Petitions such as these continued throughout the war as each branch of the church did their best to shepherd their flocks in the field. By establishing the presence of chaplains and offering regular worship services, influential believers like Jackson were able to spread their message of the path to salvation, while simultaneously providing their troops with a spiritual comfort zone. This ultimately aided them in dealing with the rigors and horrors of war. And by putting his trust in God, this general was able to inspire those under him to rise to all occasions and overcome all adversities that came upon them. With total confidence, Jackson routinely bragged of their bravery saying, "Who could not conquer with such troops as these?"

Even today, we can draw inspirational from the good General's example. The study of scripture is essential in maintaining a strong sense of faith in our Lord and Savior. Just like "Stonewall" Jackson, we too can stand tall, strengthening our hearts, minds, and spirit by exercising them daily with the word of God. *(NOTE: A 365-day study guide for reading the bible in one year has been included in the back of this book.)*

# Peace Be With You

On April 9, 1865, after four long years of fighting, General Robert E. Lee gracefully submitted the control of his Confederate forces to Union General Ulysses S. Grant at the village of Appomattox Court House in Virginia. By the end of May, all of the remaining Southern forces laid down their arms, bringing to conclusion one of the worst trials in American history and reuniting a country that had been divided in a great Civil War. One of the most interesting, yet often overlooked aspects of the surrender, is the intimate correspondence exchanged by both the North and South's supreme commanders over a three-day period. After discussing the matter via couriers, both generals agreed to gather together for a meeting that initiated the end of the bloodiest conflict in the nation's history. Below are some excerpts taken from their dispatches:

April 7th, 1865

*General: The results of the last week must convince you of the hopelessness of further resistance on the part of the Army of Northern Virginia in this struggle. I feel that it is so and regard it as my duty to shift from myself the responsibility of any further effusion of blood by asking of you the surrender of that portion of the Confederate States army known as the Army of Northern Virginia. - U.S. Grant, Lieutenant-General*

*General: I have received your note of this date. Though not entertaining the opinion you express of the hopelessness of further resistance on the part of the Army of Northern Virginia, I reciprocate your desire to avoid useless effusion of blood and therefore, before considering your proposition, ask the terms you will offer on condition of its surrender. - R.E. Lee, General.*

April 8th, 1865

*General: Your note of last evening in reply to mine of the same date, asking the conditions on which I will accept the surrender of the Army of Northern Virginia, is just received. In reply I would say that, peace being my great desire... I will meet you, or will designate officers to meet any officers you may name for the same purpose, at any point agreeable to you, for the purpose of arranging definitely the terms upon which the surrender of the Army of Northern Virginia will be received. - U.S. Grant, Lieutenant-General*

*General: I received at a late hour your note of today. In mine of yesterday I did not intend to propose the surrender of the Army of Northern Virginia, but to ask the terms of your proposition... I cannot, therefore, meet you with a view to surrender the Army of Northern Virginia; but as far as your proposal may affect the Confederate States forces under my command and tend to the restoration of peace, I should be pleased to meet you at 10 A.M. tomorrow on the old state road to Richmond, between the picket-lines of the two armies.* - *R.E. Lee, General.*

April 9th, 1865

*General: Your note of yesterday is received. I have not authority to treat on the subject of peace. The meeting proposed for 10 A.M. today could lead to no good. I will state, however, that I am equally desirous for peace with yourself and the whole North entertains the same feeling. The terms upon which peace can be had are well understood. By the South laying down their arms, they would hasten that most desirable event, save thousands of human lives and hundreds of millions of property not yet destroyed...* - *U.S. Grant, Lieutenant-General*

*General: I received your note of this morning on the picket-line, whither I had come to meet you and ascertain definitely what terms were embraced in your proposal of yesterday with reference to the surrender of this army. I now ask an interview, in accordance with the offer contained in your letter of yesterday, for that purpose.* - *R.E. Lee, General.*

Soon after this last dispatch, both commanders agreed (via messenger) to meet at the house of Wilmer McLean. Upon arriving first, General Lee was asked to wait in a large sitting room on the first floor of the residence. General Grant arrived shortly thereafter and entered the room alone while his staff respectfully waited on the front lawn. After apologizing for both his tardiness and ragged appearance, Grant began the conversation by saying, "I met you once before, General Lee, while we were serving in Mexico... I have always remembered your appearance and I think I should have recognized you anywhere." "Yes," replied General Lee, "I know I met you on that occasion and I have often thought of it and tried to recollect how you looked, but I have never been able to recall a single feature."

The two veterans talked a bit more about Mexico and moved on to a discussion of the terms of the surrender when Lee asked Grant to commit the terms to paper. At a little before 4 o'clock, General Lee shook hands with General Grant, bowed to the other officers and left the room. He then exited the house and signaled to his orderly to bring up his horse. As Lee mounted, Grant stepped down from the porch and, moving toward him, saluted him by raising his hat. All of the Union officers present followed him in this act of courtesy. Lee returned the gesture and rode off to break the sad news to the men he had commanded for so long.

Years later, the generals met for the last time. Ulysses S. Grant had entered the world of politics and was elected 18th president of the United States. Robert E. Lee was the acting president of Washington University. Neither man wished to reminisce and avoided discussing the war. Their desire was to accept the results as God's will and move on together in peace.

It is ironic, that the legacy left behind by both of these peaceful men remains entirely rooted in their service during the Civil War. Despite their many contributions that followed the surrender at Appomattox Court House, both generals Grant and Lee will always be remembered as first, and foremost, war fighters.

# The Fighting Irish

According to the doctrine of the Catholic faith, one of the most important duties that a priest performs is administering the act of Last Rites. It is a form of absolution given to a dying person. In times of war, men would obviously fall on the battlefield without the benefit of having a priest nearby. In order to accommodate this unfortunate circumstance, Catholic chaplains performed a universal form of the ritual of Last Rites prior to the battle. Much like their Protestant peers, the Catholics gathered together on the eve of (or hours before) an anticipated engagement for a religious service. The ceremony included the administering of "Last Rites," granting general absolution to all who were present, in the event that some of them were killed on the battlefield later.

This service was especially important to brigades that were composed of immigrants of Irish and German extraction. Perhaps the most famous of these was the "Irish Brigade," who deployed with Father William Corby. The *American Civil War* Web site describes his invaluable service stating, "For many Civil War soldiers, both North and South, religion served to provide hope and meaning, given what they endured during this bloody, violent conflict. When possible, men of the church would take an active role in lending such to the troops both during times of idleness and of combat."

They add, "The Reverend Father William Corby, chaplain to the Union's 'Irish Brigade' among others, extended general absolution to all soldiers, Catholic and non-Catholic alike. He was also known to administer Last Rites to the dying on the field while under fire. Prior to the conflict in the Wheatfield on the second day of the Battle of Gettysburg, he offered general absolution to the Irish Brigade. Despite the loss of 506 of their men during that day's battle, one soldier stated that, because of Father Corby, he felt as strong as a lion after that and felt no fear although his comrade was shot down beside him. Not the only example of heroism by people of the clergy, Chaplain William Hoge ignored the Union Blockade to bring Bibles to Southern soldiers."

Father Corby was born in Detroit, Michigan, on October 2, 1833, to Daniel and Elizabeth Corby. Daniel was a native of King's County, Ireland and Elizabeth was a citizen of Canada. Daniel became a prominent real estate dealer and one of the wealthiest landowners in the country. He also helped to found many parishes in Detroit and build many churches. His son William attended the common schools until he was sixteen and then joined his father's business for four years. Daniel realized that William had a calling to the priesthood and a desire to go to college, so he sent him and his two younger brothers to the ten-year-old University of Notre Dame in South Bend, Indiana. The Congregation of the Holy Cross staffed the school then, as they continue to today.

After graduation, William Corby returned to the school and became a faculty member. During the Civil War, he volunteered his services as a chaplain in the Union Army at the request of Father Sorin, who was the superior-general of the Congregation of the Holy Cross. Corby resigned his professorship at Notre Dame and was assigned as chaplain to the 88th New York Volunteer Infantry in the famed "Irish Brigade" of Thomas Francis Meagher. It has been written that he boarded the train with a song on his lips—singing, "I'll hang my harp on a willow tree. I'm off to the wars again: A peaceful home has no charm for me. The battlefield no pain."

For the next three years, Father Corby ministered to the troops with great enthusiasm, making him popular with the men. According to the Catholic Cultural Society, "Chaplains, like officers, won the common soldiers' respect with their bravery under fire. Father Corby's willingness to share the hardships of the men with a light-hearted attitude and his calm heroism in bringing spiritual and physical comfort to men in the thick of the fighting won him the esteem and the friendship of the men he served. Frequently under fire, Corby moved among casualties on the field, giving assistance to the wounded and absolution to the dying. For days after the battles, he inhabited the field hospitals to bring comfort to men in pain."

Known for their glorious (and disastrous) charge at Fredericksburg, the "Irish Brigade" also made a gallant stand at Gettysburg, where their priest has been forever memorialized in a modest statue that stands near the Pennsylvania Monument. The Catholic Cultural Society describes a defining moment for both the brigade and their chaplain by recalling, "Before the Brigade engaged the Confederate soldiers at a wheat field just south of Gettysburg, Father William Corby, in a singular event that lives in the history of the Civil War, addressed the troops. Placing his purple stole around his neck, Corby climbed atop a large boulder and offered absolution to the entire unit, a ceremony never before performed in America.

[L.F.] Kohl, editor of Corby's memoirs, tells us that Father Corby sternly reminded the soldiers of their duties, warning that the Church would deny a proper Christian burial to any that wavered and did not uphold the flag. The members of the Brigade were admonished to confess their sins in the correct manner at their earliest opportunity." At the end of the day, 198 of the men whom Father Corby had blessed had been killed.

After the war, in 1865, Father Corby returned to the university at Notre Dame where he was made vice president. Within a year, he was named president of the institution, and at the end of his term in 1872, Father Corby was sent to Sacred Heart College. He returned to Notre Dame as president in 1877 where he became known as the "Second Founder of Notre Dame" for his successful effort in rebuilding the campus following a devastating fire. Later he became assistant-general for the worldwide order.

Father Corby wrote a book of his recollections entitled "Memoirs of Chaplain Life." He stated, "Oh, you of a younger generation, think of what it cost our forefathers to save our glorious inheritance of union and liberty! If you let it slip from your hands you will deserve to be branded as ungrateful cowards and undutiful sons. But, no! You will not fail to cherish the prize—it is too sacred a trust—too dearly purchased."

He died in 1897 and as he was being buried, surviving veterans of the Grand Army of the Republic sang this song: "Answering the call of roll on high. Dropping from the ranks as they make reply. Filling up the army of the by and by."

# Chaplains In The Confederacy

Most people are familiar with the importance of religion in the day-to-day life of General Thomas "Stonewall" Jackson. However, they may not be aware of the considerable role he played in the implementation and promotion of religion during the Civil War.

In addition to being one of the Confederate Army's most fearsome commanders, Jackson was also very instrumental in the establishment of military-based chaplains in the field. As a devout evangelical Christian, he was actively religious and held the civilian position as a deacon in the Lexington Presbyterian Church. He practiced his faith through devotions and Bible study wherever he went. Though obligated to do so, he profoundly disliked fighting on Sundays.

Much to Jackson's dismay, most armies during the War Between the States did not commonly deploy with embedded clergy. Clearly, this Christian general recognized the need for spiritual strengthening and realized a healthy soul meant healthy troops. He was one of the South's first high-ranking officers to personally lobby for chaplains, arguing that a soldier's mental state of mind directly affected his ability to perform on the battlefield. Jackson also regularly put forth an effort to introduce this philosophy to the rest of the Confederate Army.

After acknowledging a lack of participation in the war effort by the church, Jackson sent a adamant-sounding letter to the Southern Presbyterian General Assembly, petitioning them for support. In it he stated, "Each branch of the Christian Church should send into the army some of its most prominent ministers who are distinguished for their piety, talents and zeal; and such ministers should labor to produce concert of action among chaplains and Christians in the army. These ministers should give special attention to preaching to regiments which are without chaplains and induce them to take steps to get chaplains, to let the regiments name the denominations from which they desire chaplains selected and then to see that suitable chaplains are secured." He added, "A bad selection of a chaplain may prove a curse instead of a blessing."

Despite the lack of readily available clergymen in the early Confederate Army, Jackson appointed a personal minister to his staff and maintained daily prayer rituals whether in camp or on the march. Whenever possible, a strict schedule of morning and evening worship on the Sabbath, as well as Wednesday prayer meetings, was adhered to with all due diligence. One of the local Fredericksburg preachers, the chaplain Reverend Tucker Lacy, of the Presbyterian Church, routinely led the services, which were often attended by General Lee and his staff.

As the courageous reputation of the "Stonewall Brigade" continued to grow, so did its quest for salvation. Jackson's steadfast faith and passion for sharing the Word ultimately inspired his men to rise to the occasion and his beliefs became infectious throughout the ranks. By putting his trust in God, he was able to inspire those under him to achieve victory in the face of defeat. With total confidence, he routinely bragged of their bravery saying, "Who could not conquer with such troops as these?"

In addition, Reverend Lacy's energizing speeches quickly became a popular event for saved and unsaved soldiers alike, who attended his sermons by the thousands. Jackson recalled one particular event that summarized the success of their ministry. He wrote, "It was a noble sight to see there those, who led our armies to victory and upon whom the eyes of the nation are turned with admiration and gratitude, melted in tears at the story of the cross and the exhibition of the love of God to the repenting and returned sinner."

Thanks to the good general's efforts and example, the Confederate Army soon began assigning chaplains to accompany its flocks into the field. Some of these shepherds even went so far as to participate in the fight, but most were stationed at camp for weekly rituals and ceremonies before and after the battle. As expected, there were predominantly Protestant preachers in the South. The Catholic contingency was larger in the North's ranks, mostly due to the large population of immigrants.

Regardless of the balance of Protestants and Catholics, denominations were not important in the eyes of Jackson or his peers. He specifically addressed this issue by stating, "Denominational distinctions should be kept out of view and not touched upon. And, as a general rule, I do not think a chaplain who would preach denominational sermons should be in the army. His congregation is his regiment and it is composed of various denominations. I would like to see no question asked in the army of what denomination a chaplain belongs to; but let the question be, does he preach the Gospel?"

As the war progressed, a movement referred to as "The Great Revival" took place in the South. Beginning in the fall of 1863, this event was in full progress throughout the Army of Northern Virginia. Before the revival was interrupted by General U.S. Grant's attack in May of 1864, approximately 7,000 soldiers (ten percent of Robert E. Lee's force) were reportedly converted. Many of these new believers came out of Stonewall's corps, who carried their message of newfound salvation home with them.

Always the teacher, Jackson dedicated almost every waking moment (that did not require his military service) to educating the uneducated, uplifting the downtrodden and introducing those around him to the glory of God. It was directly through his perseverance that other brigades in other commands benefited from the presence of clergy and that inevitably made the horrors of war a little more tolerable.

# Stonewall's Steed

Throughout the course of military history, generals have always relied on the faithful obedience and service of their troops. The fulfillment of one's duty is the prime directive of every disciplined soldier and executing orders under fire is crucial in achieving victory on the battlefield. Members of the armed forces are often called upon to follow their commanders blindly into desperate and dangerous situations without question and without hesitation. Thus is the nature of man at war.

Another loyal servant to the high command, whose contributions are overlooked, is the horse. Completely unaware of the politics, protocol and hypocrisy of war, this animal is more than just a mount. It is a faithful friend and follower who carries its commander into battle with the same bravery as the humans around it.

Many of the generals that we study today enjoyed the companionship of these valiant steeds. And in many cases, the horse's name has become almost as famous as that of its owner. This was especially true during the Civil War. In the Confederate Army, Robert E. Lee's horse, Traveller quickly became a Southern icon. In the Union Army, it was Philip Sheridan's mount, Winchester, who captured the hearts and minds of the North.

A very special horse that ultimately became as beloved as its rider was Thomas "Stonewall" Jackson's mount, Little Sorrel. No other horse, it seems, has been honored with such grace and dignity as this undersized steed. Like his commander, the story of Little Sorrel is one of both triumph and tragedy.

In 1861, Colonel Thomas J. Jackson was deployed to the most northern point of the Confederate states, at Harper's Ferry. His orders were to take command of troops from the Valley District and secure the U.S. armory and arsenal. During this time, Jackson focused on training his army, as well as the logistics required to supply and maintain it. Acquiring the horses that were essential for mobilization demanded his immediate attention.

Luckily, a few days after his arrival, an eastbound train full of livestock was seized. On board was a herd of domestic horses that was instantly recruited into the Confederacy. Obviously spooked and weary from their journey, the horses were led out of their railroad cars and taken to the nearby river for water. Jackson, without a mount at the time, approached the animals and selected two candidates with the help of Major John Harmon. One was a large, muscular stallion; the other was a smaller and rounder Morgan. At first, Jackson planned to present the little Morgan as a gift to his wife. But he grew frustrated with the larger animal, which proved to be difficult and ornery.

Within a day, the colonel had made his decision. The bigger and more powerful horse remained skittish, while the smaller sorrel had an easy gait and a pleasant temperament. Appropriately, Jackson named the horse "Little Sorrel"—creating one of the Civil War's most recognizable duos.

Jackson's most famous attribute was his unflinching bravery, which won him the nickname of "Stonewall" at the Battle of Manassas (also known as First Bull Run). A devout Presbyterian, he believed that the time of his death had already been determined, thus no place on the battlefield was any safer than the next. He said, "My religious belief teaches me to feel as safe in battle as in bed. God has fixed the time for my death. I do not concern myself about that, but to always be ready, no matter when it may overtake me."

His unwavering faith and dedication to God and country inspired his troops (later christened the "Stonewall Brigade") to charge with reckless abandon into battle and on to victory over the most dire of circumstances. It is often forgotten, but important to remember, that every time Jackson entered the battlefield, he was atop his faithful horse.

Every musket ball and exploding shell that Jackson faced was also faced by his faithful mount. Little Sorrel's service record, even for a horse, was extraordinary. Some of his milestones included the Battle of Manassas, the Seven Days Battle, the Battle of Fredericksburg and the tragic Battle of Chancellorsville. As a testament to the animal's strength of will, Henry Kyd, Jackson's staff officer, once remarked that he never observed a sign of fatigue in Little Sorrel.

Throughout the war, Jackson's horse, like his men, remained cool under fire. His troops' loyalty to their commander was second to none and his bravery became infectious throughout the ranks. Due to a successful defensive campaign on Southern soil, the Confederacy seemed well on its way to acquiring accepted independence.

All that changed after the sudden and accidental death of the man they called "Stonewall."

On May 2, 1863, during the Battle of Chancellorsville, Jackson's own men accidentally fired upon him. He suffered three wounds and had to have an arm amputated. Initially, Jackson looked to make a full recovery, but he later developed an incurable case of pneumonia. In the end, he clearly accepted his fate as part of God's divine plan and resolved to spend his last hours, before delirium set in, reading from the Bible.

Following the death of his master, Little Sorrel became a symbol of Southern pride and survived to a ripe old age. Jackson's widow cared for the horse until dwindling finances forced her to send him to the Virginia Military Institute. There the cadets looked after their ex-instructor's mount until he relocated once again to the Confederate veterans' home in Richmond.

Little Sorrel toured as an attraction at country fairs and attended many reunions for Civil War veterans. It has also been written that Southern ladies would sometimes clip hairs from his mane and tail to make wristlets and rings. At the tender age of 33, Little Sorrel was a bona fide celebrity sideshow. In 1884, he was photographed with an 85-year-old Confederate soldier named Napoleon Hull, who was said to have been the oldest surviving veteran of Jackson's army.

Unfortunately, like "Stonewall," the retired horse would also suffer a tragic demise at the hands of "his own men."

Eventually, the animal's rapidly deteriorating health became crippling. Confederate veterans rigged a makeshift sling to hoist him to his feet whenever visitors arrived. One day, the sling accidentally slipped off and the poor horse fell to the floor, breaking his back. Death came shortly thereafter.

After the passing of Little Sorrel in 1886, CSA veterans had his hide mounted and preserved, where it remains on display in the VMI Museum. He is one of only two horses ever to be preserved from the Civil War. The other horse is Sheridan's Winchester.

According to an article printed in the *Washington Times*, "At the time, standard taxidermy practice was to use the bones and ligaments of an animal. However, in large animals such as a horse, skin deterioration ensued. The technician in charge was Frederic S. Webster, with a studio on Pennsylvania Avenue in Washington D.C. Webster had previously been employed at 'Prof. Henry A. Ward's Scientific Establishment' in Rochester, N.Y., and had participated in the mounting of [Gen. Philip H. Sheridan's mount]."

The taxidermist who handled the animal's carcass took the bones as a partial payment and later donated them to the Carnegie Museum in Pittsburgh, Pennsylvania. This was something that never sat right with southerners. Eventually, the institute retrieved the horse's frame.

On July 20, 1997, 111 years later, the animal's skeleton was finally cremated and his ashes were scattered beneath the famous bronze statue of his master at the entrance to the Virginia Military Institute. The reburial and ceremony were due to the efforts of the Virginia Division of the United Daughters of the Confederacy and echoed the pageantry of days gone by.

Complete with mounted cavalry and infantry, a fife and drum corps, a bagpiper, and ladies in period dress, Little Sorrel's bones were escorted to his grave in a special 18-inch-tall walnut casket created for the event.

As Jackson would have wanted, the invocation, blessing and benediction were offered by the Reverend William Klein, pastor of Lexington Presbyterian Church, where Jackson and his wife, Mary Anna Morrison, had worshipped. Other prominent speakers included Dr. James I. Robertson, author of the recently published definitive biography of Little Sorrel's master, and Colonel Keith Gibson, the director of the school's museum.

To this day, Little Sorrel remains a symbol of bravery and service, not only to the cadets at VMI, but to all who pay tribute to the men who fought in battle—and the animals that carried them there.

# THE Christian General

Much like his Confederate counterparts, Union General Oliver Otis Howard personified the Christian Soldier. Even in battle Howard was as much a moral crusader as a warrior, insisting that his troops attend prayer and temperance meetings. A documentary that was aired on the Public Broadcasting Service entitled "The Civil War," summed up the life of the Yankee commander perfectly by stating, "Throughout his long military career, Oliver Howard gained victory by the force of his moral convictions, as often as by force of arms."

In 1857, Howard was a full-time soldier who was deployed to Florida for the Seminole Wars. It was there that he experienced a conversion to evangelical Christianity and considered resigning from the army to become a minister. His religious proclivities would later earn him the nickname "the Christian general." Upon the outbreak of the American Civil War, Howard, an opponent of slavery, resigned his regular army commission and became the colonel of the 3rd Maine Volunteers in the Union Army. Much like "Stonewall" Jackson, Howard made spiritual strengthening a daily part of his troop's routine.

As the war progressed, a movement referred to as "The Great Revival" took place in the South. Beginning in the fall of 1863, this event was in full progress throughout the Army of Northern Virginia. Before the revival was interrupted by Grant's attack in May of 1864, approximately 7,000—ten percent of Lee's force—were reportedly converted. Doctor Gardiner H. Shattuck, Jr., author of *A Shield and Hiding Place: The Religious Life of the Civil War Armies*, reports that "The best estimates of conversions in the Union forces place the figure between 100,000 and 200,000 men—about five to ten percent of all individuals engaged in the conflict. In the smaller Confederate armies, at least 100,000 were converted. Since these numbers include only "conversions" and do not represent the number of soldiers actually swept up in the revivals—a yet more substantial figure—the impact of revivals during the Civil War surely was tremendous."

According to some accounts, in the early stages of the war, revivals like the one Howard led were not the rule, but the exception. By most appearances, religion had not left home with the soldiers. The magazine *Christianity Today* recalled the trials and tribulations associated with trying to live a devout life while on campaign. It stated: "Day-to-day army life was so boring that men were often tempted to 'make some foolishness,' as one soldier typified it. Profanity, gambling, drunkenness, sexual licentiousness and petty thievery confronted those who wanted to practice their faith. Christians complained that no Sabbath was observed. Despite the efforts of a few generals like George McClellan and Oliver O. Howard, ordinary routines went on as if Sunday meant nothing at all. General Robert McAllister, an officer who was working closely with the United States Christian Commission, complained that a 'tide of irreligion' had rolled over his army 'like a mighty wave.'"

Unfortunately, Howard's motivational efforts did not always result in victory on the battlefield in the same manner as those of "Stonewall" Jackson. At the Battle of Fair Oaks (in June of 1862) he was wounded twice in the right arm. The second round shattered the bone near the elbow. The arm was amputated and Howard spent two months recovering from his wounds before returning to active duty. He was given the Medal of Honor as a result of his gallantry.

An August 1864 issue of *Harper's Weekly* reported that "General Howard has lost his right arm in his country's service. It used to be a joke between him and [General Philip] Kearney, who had lost his left arm, that, as a matter of economy, they might purchase their gloves together." One of Howard's most significant moments in the field came at Gettysburg, when he assumed command of Major-General John Reynolds' troops after Reynolds was killed.

After the war, he was appointed head of the Freedman's Bureau, which was formed to protect and assist the newly freed slaves. Many Southerners, as well as some Northerners, harshly criticized Howard for his unapologetic support of black suffrage and the distribution of land to African-Americans. He fearlessly expressed his belief that the majority of white Southerners would be happy to see a return to slavery. He supported freedom and equality for former slaves in his private life, by working to make his elite Washington, D.C. church racially integrated. He also helped to found an all-black college in the District of Columbia, which was named Howard University in his honor.

In addition, Howard was active in Indian affairs, engagements and subsequent relations in the West and is remembered as a man of his word and one who maintained strong moral convictions. As was quite common, many of the surviving commanders of the Civil War became "celebrities" in the public eye and they often signed autographs. Howard routinely signed his with the phrase, "The Lord Is My Shepherd."

A talented writer, Howard also wrote several books including *Chief Joseph* (1881), *Zachary Taylor* (1892), *Autobiography of Oliver Otis Howard* (1907) and *Famous Indian Chiefs I Have Known* (1908). All sold well.

In tribute to the man, a bust of Howard designed by artist James E. Kelly is on display at Howard University. An impressive equestrian statue depicting Howard in action stands on East Cemetery Hill on the Gettysburg Battlefield and a dormitory at Bowdoin College has been named for Howard.

Much like his Confederate counterpart, Thomas "Stonewall" Jackson, Oliver Howard is to be credited for his evangelistic efforts on behalf of the North, in addition to his activism on behalf of all minorities living in the United States at the time. He was a man of God, who ultimately became a man of the people—all people—regardless of the color of their skin.

# Stonewall's Sabbath School

It would be completely negligent not to historically acknowledge the moral dilemma over the South's practice of slavery and the contradiction that it posed in the consciences of some of its most pious citizens, including Thomas Jackson. Over the years many theologians and historians have examined this contradiction in morals, and many have concluded that fervent believers like Jackson felt that slavery was (at the time) according to God's will. In other words, they were not entirely opposed to it.

Jackson's family owned six slaves in the late 1850s. Three of them (a woman named Hetty and her teenaged sons, Cyrus and George), were received as wedding presents. Another slave, named Albert, requested that Jackson purchase him and allow him to work for his freedom. He was employed as a waiter in one of the Lexington hotels and Jackson contracted him to VMI. Another, named Amy, also requested that Jackson purchase her from a public auction. She served the family as a cook and housekeeper. The sixth, Emma, was a four-year-old orphan with a learning disability and was accepted by Jackson from an aged widow and presented to his second wife, Anna. He also had a manservant that he employed at the start of the war. This gentleman acted as a cook and valet and accompanied him into the field.

In *Stonewall Jackson: The Man, the Soldier, the Legend,* Dr. James Robertson wrote of Jackson's view on slavery. He stated, "Jackson neither apologized for nor spoke in favor of the practice of slavery." He added that Jackson believed that God had sanctioned the institution, and man had no moral right to challenge its existence. Rather he felt that the good Christian slaveholder was one who treated his servants fairly and humanely at all times.

Regardless of one's verdict with regard to "Stonewall's" feelings on the matter, we cannot deny the fact that he was very aware that all people were welcomed at the Lord's Table. Jackson was instrumental in the organization, in 1855, of Sunday school classes for blacks at the Presbyterian Church. The pastor, Dr. William Spottswood White, described the relationship between Jackson and his Sunday afternoon students: "In their religious instruction he succeeded wonderfully. His discipline was systematic and firm, but very kind. ... His servants reverenced and loved him, as they would have done a brother or father. ... He was emphatically the black man's friend." He addressed his students by name and they referred to him affectionately as "Marse Major."

Eager to share his renewed faith with all people, Jackson operated his controversial Sunday school in Lexington for African-Americans and proudly practiced the sin of civil disobedience, while teaching black children the ways of salvation. Although he could not alter the social status of slaves, he committed himself to Christian decency and pledged to "assist the souls of those held in bondage." Believing that slavery was according to God's will, he confided in some of his black students that when the time was right, they would be free.

He continued his prayerful and financial support for the rest of his life and stayed in touch with the school even when on campaign. In a letter sent to his pastor he wrote, "In my tent last night, after a fatiguing day's service, I remembered that I failed to send a contribution for our colored Sunday school. Enclosed you will find a check for that object, which please acknowledge at your earliest convenience and oblige yours faithfully."

Not surprisingly, the "minority-focused" school was highly contested and not popular with the local white citizens. It appeared that even the great "Stonewall" Jackson was susceptible to public scrutiny. Throughout the massive level of media coverage that followed Jackson's passing, most publications left out this endeavor entirely and few mentioned any of his public service with regard to African-Americans. One newspaper, *The Herald*, did recall the affection that his manservant held for the departed general. (Note the blatant use of racist slang for quotes)

It printed: "He had in his service, a Negro who had become so used to his ways as to know when he was about to start on an expedition without receiving any notice from his master. When asked how he could know that, as his master never talked about his plans, the Negro answered, 'Massa Jackson allers prays ebery night and ebery mornin'; but when he go on any expedishum he pray two, or tree, or four times durin' de night. When I see him pray two, or tree, or four times durin' de night, I pack de baggage, for I know he goin' on an expedishum.'"

Following Jackson's burial, Colonel J.T.L. Preston, a Lexington attorney who first suggested and actively promoted the establishment of the Virginia Military Institute, continued Jackson's ministry. The school remained in operation as a testament to the general's grace and charity. Today, several descendants of the first students to attend this school have acknowledged "Stonewall's" part in introducing their ancestors to the teachings of the Bible. In this regard, we can see how the evangelical white Christian slave owner can (and often did) have a positive influence on the future of those held in bondage. For example, many ex-slave preachers were responsible for some of the largest revivals that followed the Civil War and many routinely gave sermons to white congregations. Some even preached to the Virginia Legislature on more than one occasion.

These aspects are often overlooked (or scoffed at) by non-believers and historical skeptics who choose to examine the institution of slavery in purely secular terms. For devout believers who view the world through non-secular eyes, the idea of showing compassion, mercy and fulfilling an obligation to "make disciples of all nations" reinforces why one would go to such lengths to both educate and enlighten slaves. Simply put, Jackson did exactly what his Lord had told him to do: he spread the Good News.

# Guidance And Grace

Following his graduation from the military academy at West Point, Second Lieutenant James Ewell Brown Stuart received a commission into the Mounted Rifles and orders for deployment to the Midwestern territories. Rapidly adapting to his new duties and surroundings, Stuart immediately showed the potential to be a fine commanding officer. It was during this period that he became more intimate in his relationship with God.

Although he was by no means a "Bible Thumper," often he would participate in scripture study with his fellow Christian troopers and his dedication to the reading the Word of God grew more each day. In retrospect, perhaps both the desolate location of his post and the lack of distractions may have played a big part in Stuart's salvation. If an idle mind really is "the Devil's Workshop," he certainly kept his mind busy.

His maturing demeanor and strict code of ethics also helped maintain an obedient lifestyle, free from disruption. As a young boy, Stuart pledged to his mother that he would avoid the "ills of man," including alcohol, tobacco and gambling. Amazingly, the horseman is said to have maintained this vow for the entire course of his life and only drank whiskey (a medicinal painkiller) on his last day at the insistence of his physician. This commitment and willpower signified his spiritual strength and his loyalty to the Lord helped to guide him.

Stuart also remained thoughtful of his family and church back home. At one point, he wrote to his mother with regard to financially supporting the development of a house of worship on the family's property saying, "I wish to devote one hundred dollars to the purchase of a comfortable log church near your place, because in all my observation I believe one is more needed in that neighborhood than any other that I know of; and besides, 'charity begins at home.' Seventy-five of this one hundred dollars I have in trust for that purpose and the remainder is my own contribution. If you will join me with twenty-five dollars, a contribution of a like amount from two or three others interested will build a very respectable free church. What will you take for the south half of your plantation? I want to buy it."

During his time on the plains, Stuart and the U.S. Cavalry were involved in pre-emptive actions against what were referred to as potential hostiles.

In an effort to preserve peace and safety between the new settlers in Kansas Territory and the occupying Native American tribes, the mounted army filled the position of a disciplinary body, maintaining order over both settlers and Indians. At the time, whether Kansas would be considered a free or slave state was still undetermined. This uncertainty eventually led to political stress and social disorder.

One particular campaign during Stuart's deployment involved a battle fought at the North Fork of the Solomon River and resulted in the cavalier sustaining a serious wound. On July 29, 1857, his superior, Colonel Sumner, led six companies of mounted rifleman against nearly 300 Cheyenne warriors. After initially attacking, the Indian forces fell back, forcing a relentless pursuit by the troopers. Stuart initially led the chase for more than five miles, but eventually his horse became exhausted, requiring him to pull back. After allowing the animal to catch its breath, Stuart forged ahead and attempted to exchange his winded steed with one from a subordinate. While doing so, he came upon a group of men engaged in deadly hand-to-hand combat.

He later recalled the incident: "When I overtook the rear of the enemy I found Lomax in imminent peril from an Indian, who was on foot and in the act of shooting him. I rushed to the rescue and succeeded in wounding the Indian in his thigh. He fired at me in return with an Allen's revolver, but missed. I now observed Stanley and McIntyre close by. The former said, 'Wait! I'll fetch him.' He dismounted from his horse to aim deliberately, but in dismounting accidentally discharged his last load. Upon him the Indian now advanced with his revolver pointed. I could not stand that, but drawing my saber rushed on the monster and inflicted a severe wound across his head; but at the same moment he fired his last barrel within a foot of me, the ball taking effect in the center of the breast, but, by the mercy of God, glancing to the left, lodging near my nipple and so far inside that it cannot be felt."

Upon assessing the loss and burying his casualties, Colonel Sumner continued the pursuit of the retreating Indians southward. Falling further behind by the hour, he finally decided to leave his wounded men (including Lieutenant Stuart) in a temporary fortification built near the battlefield and garrisoned by one company of infantry. Despite suffering great pain, Stuart acknowledged his Savior and repeatedly offered prayers of gratitude for his survival. (This would become a recurring theme as he escaped more than his share of deadly and desperate situations in the years to come.)

After several days—and much prayerful consideration—a bleeding Stuart was somehow able to mount his horse and set out to find assistance. Miraculously, the weakened and delirious trooper found a deserted route back to an Army post where he obtained medical aid for those left behind. He later credited God alone for guiding him on his precarious journey. He wrote to his dear wife, assuring her of his successful recovery. Under the care of Dr. Charles Brewer, the regimental surgeon, Stuart was moved to a safer location that allowed him an opportunity to meditate on his good fortune. Still, his restlessness was apparent.

In his letter to his beloved Flora Cooke, he stated: "I rejoice to inform you that the wound is not regarded as dangerous, though I may be confined to my bed for weeks. I am now enjoying excellent health in every other aspect. We have a pretty view up the creek for about two miles. I can sit up a little with props and seize a moment now and then to jot a daily token to my wife. The day drags heavily. My Prayer Book—which I must say has not been neglected—and my Army Regulations are my only books. A few sheets of *Harper's Weekly* are treasures indeed."

Flora's husband later made a full recovery and returned to her side with a renewed sense of faith. Divine Intervention had led him through the darkest of times, only to reveal a light that would continue to shine on the cavalier. Clearly God's grace had saved him. His providence had spared him. Perhaps He even had a plan for Stuart—a purpose yet unfulfilled—one that would come during one of the darkest times in our nation's history.

# Lincoln's Legacy

Neither party expected for the war, the magnitude, or the duration, which it has already attained. Neither anticipated that the cause of the conflict might cease with, or even before, the conflict itself should cease. Each looked for an easier triumph, and a result less fundamental and astounding. Both read the same Bible, and pray to the same God; and each invokes His aid against the other. It may seem strange that any men should dare to ask a just God's assistance in wringing their bread from the sweat of other men's faces; but let us judge not, that we be not judged. The prayers of both could not be answered; that of neither has been answered fully. The Almighty has His own purposes.

– President Abraham Lincoln's Second Inaugural Address, March 4, 1865

# *soldier's sermon*

The following transcript has been provided courtesy of Chaplain Alan Farley, curator of the National Civil War Chaplain's Research Center and Museum and founder of the Re-enactor's Missions for Jesus Christ: www.rmjc.org.

# A Sermon For The Soldier

By the Reverend J. A. Proctor

I presume you have a leisure hour. If so, it may be interesting to you to peruse a few thoughts which I purpose to set down in simple language and address to you. Every soldier of our Confederacy is an object of great interest to those for whom he is fighting. Sometimes the soldier is disposed to doubt this. Letters from home come but seldom; his name is not mentioned in the newspaper; he sees himself as only one of a great multitude, "lost like a drop in the boundless main," and he concludes that he is uncared for and well-nigh forgotten. Soldier, this is not so. There are but few in our whole country who are not anxiously concerned in regard to your condition. Compared with our entire population, there are but few heartless speculators, and there are hardly any whose hearts are in sympathy with the Yankee Government. All the rest of our people feel a constant solicitude for the brave soldiers who are enduring hardships, and fearlessly facing the dangers of the battle-field, in defence of Southern honor and Southern rights. They are concerned for your bodily condition. When they meet around the table to share the food with which a kind Providence has supplied them, they think of your scanty and hard fare, and would joyfully divide their portion with you. When the wintry winds are howling around their dwellings, and the rain pours down in torrents, or the snow is covering the earth and chilling the air, they remember the poor soldiers who are exposed to it all, and would gladly protect them from the storm. To hear that any of our soldiers are without blankets, or clothing or shoes, sends a pang to every true Southrons heart. Our people know that you have enough to suffer even when best provided for, and I am very greatly mistaken if they will not do all in their power to make your condition as comfortable as your circumstances will admit.

But, soldier, your people at home are not merely concerned for your bodily condition, they are concerned for your moral and spiritual welfare. Not all, it is true, who are interested in your physical well-being are careful of your religious condition, but there are thousands at home who feel the deepest interest in this subject, while they are not forgetful of the former. There are *mothers* here who, in the fear of God and in the faith of the Gospel, are sending up earnest prayers to heaven for the sons whom God has given them. They are praying not only that God may protect their boys in the day of battle and from the diseases of the camp, but that He will preserve them from the vices of the army, and make them upright, honorable, high-minded Christian men. *Soldier, have you a mother?* There are fathers and sisters here, who have brothers and sons in the field, believe in God, that daily and fervently pray for God's spiritual blessings on their brothers and sons in the army; and the Church of Christ, in all its branches, feels this solicitude pressing on its great heart a mighty weight of responsibility. From every congregation in the land, fervent supplications for blessings on the army are sent up every Sabbath; and in the stillness of the closet, at morning, noon and evening of every day, the prayers of the Sabbath are earnestly repeated. Societies have been organized for the especial purpose of promoting the religious interests of the soldier; holy, God-fearing men have been employed to act as colporteurs, and thousands of religious tracts are being daily distributed in the hospitals and in the camps. It is a matter of devout thanksgiving to Almighty God that all this interest has not been manifested in vain. Cheering accounts of religious revivals come in from almost every department of the army. It is not extravagant to say that thousands of soldiers, who were unconcerned before, have been converted to God since this war began. Some of those are now living to adorn the doctrines of the Saviour, and some of them are filling soldiers graves; but they died in the triumphs of a Saviours love.

Soldier, you have witnessed this interest in your spiritual welfare. You have seen the colporteur in his daily rounds, and you have read some of the tracts; but let me ask you how has the exhibition of this interest on the part of your friends at home affected you?

The writer of these lines is to you, soldier, an unknown stranger. Your eyes and his, it is probable, never met. You may never see him until the conflicts and storms of worldly life are over. But as he writes these lines he feels the sympathies of a common kindred, and his heart moves within him in strong desire to do you good. Come, then, and let us reason together, for a little season, on this most important concern that relates to man. I shall ask you one question, which I hope you will patiently consider. I can not hear your answer; but God is ever near you; His eyes behold you, and his ears understand the voiceless language of your heart.

*Are you a Christian?* Perhaps you answer, *yes.*—You look back to the time when your soul first felt the peace of God. It was a happy day. If I were with you to-day it would give me pleasure to hear you recount the comforts of that blest occasion. It is well to speak often of the time of our conversion. If we have no hearers who will take an interest in the story, we should at least meditate upon it in our own hearts. If you have been in God's service long, you have no doubt often felt refreshed by singing that sweet hymn of Dr. Doddridge, beginning:

*Oh, happy day that fixed my choice*
*On Thee, my Saviour and my God.*
*Well may this glowing heart rejoice,*
*And tell its raptures all abroad.*

It must be especially pleasant to the soldier who was converted at home to call up the memory of that day. He goes back to the church where his fathers worshipped—"forms and faces" of dearly loved ones, which perhaps "he shall see no more," stand up before him, and crowd around him—and for a moment he imagines that the war is ended and the endearing associations of former life returned. But my friend let me call you away from this pleasing meditation, to remind you that you have had many strong temptations and many terrible struggles with [the] enemy of souls since you first became a Christian, and to assure you that, in all probability, if you live much longer, you will have many more. Oh, be strong for the coming conflicts. Prepare yourself by reading God's holy word, frequent meditations and earnest prayers.

*The boatmans oar may pause upon the galley,*
*The soldier sleep beneath his plumed crest,*
*And peace may fold her wing oer hill and valley,*
*But thou, oh, Christian, must not take thy rest.*

As a good soldier, in your country's service, you "endure hardness"—sometimes advancing, sometimes retreating, sometimes without food and sometimes exposed storm and cold, sometimes in health and sometimes sick—but *always,* with unconquered will, your watchword is "liberty or death." So likewise, as the soldier of Jesus Christ, you must be firm and strong. Hold fast to your profession, maintain your integrity, trust in the living God. If you fall, be not utterly cast down, but rise up, and in the name of Jesus, who lives in Heaven to intercede for his tempted followers, determine to try again. May God help you, Christian soldier, to "fight the good fight of faith, and *lay hold* on eternal life!"

Perhaps your answer is, *I was once a Christian.* Poor backslider! While battling with carnal weapons against the enemy of your country, you have been unmindful of the secret stratagems of the great adversary of souls. You are to-day "led captive by Satan at his will." The "strong man armed" has bound you, and you feel powerless and helpless. I do not reproach you. If you ever reflect on the past, you have enough to oppress you without any word from man.

You remember the day of your conversion, the consolation you found in religion, the peace which passeth understanding, and the joy which is unspeakable. You remember the joy of your friends when you told them that God was gracious, and the solemn vows and promises you then made to your Heavenly Father. But what a change since then! Your vows are broken, your friends have been disappointed, the joy of your heart has ceased, and you are without hope and without God. But what will you do? It must be a hard lot to lead the life of a backslidden Christian. You cannot forget the past; your hopes of Heaven and your fears of Hell conscience—is ever at work, bringing all these things to your remembrance. What will you do? Soldier, let me lead you back to the Saviour! Like Peter, you have denied the blessed Jesus, but He looks on you to-day and says gently "come back." He is able to save you[.] He is stronger than "the strong man armed." He has saved thousands as bad as you. He is willing to save you. He died on the cross to manifest his love. David, and Peter, and thousands like them, departed from God, but coming to Jesus found him a precious Saviour still. This world can not satisfy you; it will soon be gone.—Oh, why not come back to God, so that when your flesh and heart shall fail, He may be the strength of your heart and your portion forever. If you continue as you are, your life must be miserable, and dying, you will have no hope. Oh, that our merciful God may help you to return!

But it may be, soldier, that you answer my question with this language: "I am not a Christian." What are you then? A mariner on a stormy ocean, without a compass and without a star; a pilgrim in a dreary wilderness, without a father and without a home; *a sinner born to die, and without a Saviour!* Why are you not a Christian? Perhaps you have never tried to answer that question. That you are not a Christian is not because it is not to your advantage to be one, not because you have not been invited; not because you have not had opportunity, nor because you have never felt the necessity of being Christian. Why, then, let me ask, are you not a Christian? I will answer this question for you, and I pray God that the truth which I shall now tell you may be sanctified to your good! *It is because you have been lulled into a deathlike slumber by the enemy of souls.* As the ship-master came to Jonah, so come I to you! "What meanest thou, oh, sleeper? Arise, call upon thy God!" It is passing strange that you should have lived so long in this land of Gospel light, without being greatly concerned for your soul's salvation. The earth beneath and around you, and the sky above you, have told you of God; your soul is conscious of its own existence and of its immortality, and the Bible tells you that your future eternal destiny depends upon your acceptance or rejection of the terms of the Gospel. "How is it that you have no faith?"

Soldier! let me invite you to become a Christian. You doubtless remember that you have heard this invitation before now. In the church, at home, your minister has often urged you to give your heart to God. Perhaps a fond Mother has wept over her wandering boy, and urged the same request. Sisters, fair and gentle, —oh, how you would love to hear their voices to-day! —have entreated you to be reconciled to God. You have not yielded. You are still sleeping—sinning still. Oh, put off your return to God no longer. By the shortness of time and the uncertainty of life, I urge you to repent. Many years of your time are already past, and your heart, in its throbbings, is beating your funeral march to the grave. At best you can expect the years of your pilgrimage to be only "three score years and ten." How few live out the full measure of their days! But these are times of violence. Hundreds have fallen on your right hand and on your left. You have seen them die. Neither youth nor strength could save them. The enemy still threatens. He is cruel as the grave.—Other fields must be made red with human gore, *Soldier, you may fall.* Oh, be prepared; and then, living, you will be brave—and dying, you will fall a blessed martyr! But I urge you to repent on other grounds. The love of Jesus should induce you to be religious. He loved you and gave himself for you. On the cross he suffered a bitter agony and died to redeem your soul. Will you let him die in vain? He loves you still, and is now interceding for you in Heaven. How matchless is this love,—*pleading* love for rebellious man! Oh, soldier, *believe* that he loves you! it will restrain you from sin, it will bind you to the cross, it will soothe your aching heart. I might say more to you on this interesting subject, but perhaps I have already taxed you long enough. I now commend you "to God and the word of his grace which is able to build you up and give you an inheritance among the saints in light." If you are willing to become a Christian, be not afraid that Christ will cast you off. "Whoso cometh unto me, I will in no wise cast out," is the blessed promise which he makes to every sinner. Come to him by forsaking your sins, by believing his word and trusting in it, and by earnest prayer for his atoning mercy. Now; as you read, you may give up your poor heart to God. Would you know how to approach Him? Let this be your language:

*Just as I am, without one plea,*
*But that thy blood was shed for me,*
*And that thou bidst me come to thee,*
*Oh, Lamb of God, I come!*

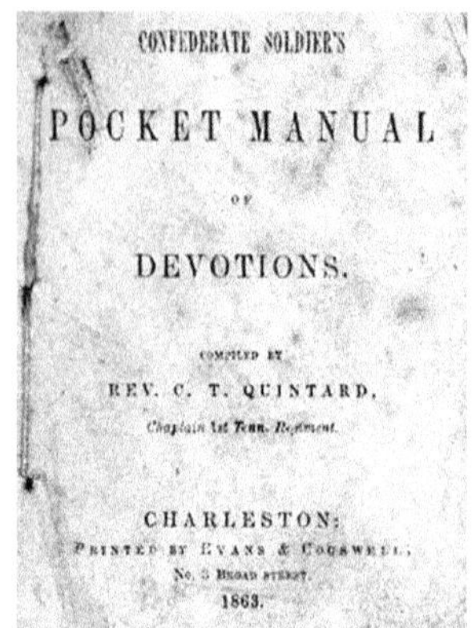

CONFEDERATE SOLDIER'S

POCKET MANUAL

OF

DEVOTIONS.

COMPILED BY

REV. C. T. QUINTARD,

Chaplain 1st Tenn. Regiment.

CHARLESTON:

PRINTED BY EVANS & COGSWELL,

No. 3 BROAD STREET.

1863.

# Religion In The Ranks

Many Confederate troops were already devout Christians at the start of the American Civil War. Thousands of others were baptized into faith during the conflict. They came from families who were strongly influenced by the camp meetings of the *Great Revival* that swept through Kentucky, Tennessee and the Carolinas in the early part of the nineteenth century. Most of the Southern soldiers were Protestants and of Methodist, Baptist, Episcopalian, or Presbyterian heritage. Many carried their own personal Bibles from home, as well as a *Prayer Book*. These pocket-sized volumes contained a collection of prayers, as well as assorted hymns and psalms. The faith that sustained them in desperate times is the same faith that supports many Christians today. The basis of that belief system is contained here in the scriptures known collectively as "*The Roman Road*."

Marching along the 'Roman Road' to salvation:

*For all have sinned, and come short of the glory of God. (Romans 3:23)*
*For the wages of sin is death; But the gift of God is eternal life through Jesus Christ our Lord. (Romans 6:23)*
*But God commendeth his love toward us, in that, while we were yet sinners, Christ died for us. (Romans 5:8)*
*That if thou shalt confess with thy mouth the Lord Jesus, and shalt believe in thine heart that God hath raised him from the dead, thou shalt be saved. (Romans 10:9)*
*For whosoever shall call upon the name of the Lord shall be saved. (Romans 10:13)*
*For with the heart man believeth unto righteousness; and with the mouth confession is made unto salvation. (Romans 10:10)*

# *faith under fire*

A tribute to the Christian commanders and soldiers of the Confederacy who fought bravely, led valiantly, and lived honorably. Though their cause was lost, their faith was never shaken.

*"May God guard and protect you and yours, and shower upon you every blessing, is the prayer of your devoted brother, R.E. LEE."*
– Excerpt of a letter from Robert E. Lee to his sister

# General Robert Edward Lee

Born: January 19, 1807, in Stratford Hall, Virginia
Died: October 12, 1870, in Lexington, Virginia
Denomination: Anglican/Episcopalian

Even today, Robert E. Lee is still considered one of the greatest commanders in the history of warfare. Early in 1861, President Lincoln offered him command of the United States forces. Though he was opposed to the secession of Virginia, Lee refused the offer. In April of 1861, Virginia seceded from the Union and Lee chose to remain loyal to his home state. As the commander of the Army of Northern Virginia, 'Marse Robert' was able to inspire and sustain a force much smaller and not as well equipped as its foe. Among his greatest victories were the Seven Days Battles, the Second Battle of Bull Run, the Battle of Fredericksburg and the Battle of Chancellorsville.

BIO: The son of Henry "Lighthorse Harry" Lee and a favorite general of George Washington, Robert Edward Lee entered the U.S. Military Academy at West Point, where he finished second in the class of 1829. In April of 1861, then Colonel Lee, declined the opportunity to command an army that was about to take the field against the seceding states. Shortly afterward, he accepted a general's position in the newly formed Confederate States Army, where he served during the first year as a senior military advisor to President Jefferson Davis. In June of 1862, Lee assumed the command of the Army of Northern Virginia, leading it to numerous victories. However, in early April of 1865, it became obvious that continued efforts would prove futile and would result in an unacceptable number of casualties and needless effusion of blood. On April 9th, General Lee met with General Ulysses S. Grant at Appomattox Courthouse in Virginia, where he surrendered the once-great army that had defended the Confederate States of America so valiantly. On October 1, 1865, he assumed the presidency of Washington College, where he continued until his death on October 12, 1870. In 1900, Lee was one of the first twenty-nine individuals selected for the Hall of Fame for Great Americans, the first Hall of Fame in the United States.

*"Our God was my shield. His protecting care is an additional cause for gratitude."*
– Thomas Jonathan Jackson

# General Thomas J. "Stonewall" Jackson

Born: January 21, 1824, in Clarksburg, (West) Virginia
Died: May 10, 1863, in Guinea Station, Virginia
Denomination: Presbyterian

Heralded, as Lee's greatest subordinate, "Old Jack" was beloved and revered in the South—detested and feared in the North. A brilliant tactician, he conducted some of the most successful military campaigns in American history. His famous "Stonewall Brigade" would have followed their commander into the depths of Hades if ordered. Jackson was also responsible for the spiritual strength of his men and initiated the formal establishment of chaplains in the Confederate Army. His Valley Campaign is still taught at America's military academies and his legacy at the Virginia Military Institute is still shared with the institution's cadets.

BIO: After rising from a childhood that was fraught with tragedy and despair, Thomas Jackson entered West Point in July of 1842, and in spite of his poor childhood education, worked hard to finish seventeenth in the Class of 1846. Following graduation, Jackson was sent to fight in the war against Mexico. In 1851, he became a professor of artillery tactics and natural philosophy at the Virginia Military Institute in Lexington. Perhaps best known as "Stonewall," Jackson earned his nickname at the First Battle of Manassas after refusing to withdraw his troops in the face of total carnage. Inspired by the bravery of his subordinate, General Barnard Bee immediately rallied the remnants of his own brigade, while shouting, "There is Jackson standing like a stone wall." Jackson later distinguished himself in the Valley Campaign, Second Manassas and the Battle of Fredericksburg. A fervent prayer warrior, his religious devotion was a constant in all facets of his life. On May 2, 1863, Jackson was wounded by friendly fire at the Battle of Chancellorsville. Despite surviving the amputation of his left arm, he developed severe pneumonia and died eight days later. His death was a severe setback for the Confederacy. Gen. Lee stated, "He has lost his left arm; I have lost my right." Today, tourists come from all over the world to visit the Stonewall Jackson Shrine and pay homage to one of America's greatest Christian soldiers.

*"I am resigned; God's will be done."*
– J.E.B. Stuart's last words

# General James Ewell Brown "J.E.B." Stuart

Born: February 6, 1833, in Patrick County, Virginia
Died: May 12, 1864, in Richmond, Virginia
Denomination: Methodist/Episcopalian

A true 'cavalier' in every sense of the term, J.E.B. Stuart was a master of reconnaissance and the use of cavalry in offensive operations. Sporting a magnificent cinnamon beard, red cape, yellow sash and a hat cocked to the side with a peacock feather, the horseman had as much flair in life as strength on the battlefield. Conducting raids and rides of epic proportions, Stuart became a 'favorite son' of General Lee, and is said to have never brought him a bad piece of information. On two different occasions he rode around Maj. Gen. George B. McClellan's army undetected; once in the Peninsula Campaign and once after the Battle of Antietam. While these two missions were not tactically significant, they became a celebratory boost to Southern morale.

BIO: James Ewell Brown Stuart was born in Patrick County, Virginia, on February 6, 1833. From 1848 to 1850, Stuart attended Emory and Henry College. In 1850, he entered the U.S. Military Academy. In the years that followed his graduation, he received various commissions for exemplary service in Texas, Kansas, and Washington. Following the secession of his beloved home state of Virginia in 1861, Stuart resigned his commission in the U.S. Army and was appointed to serve as a cavalry commander under Thomas "Stonewall" Jackson. According to General Robert E. Lee, Stuart was an ideal soldier and because of his tremendous riding skills and sharp instincts as an intelligence officer, Lee regarded him as the "eyes of the army." Dramatic in his appearance, Stuart always rode a grand horse, lined his gray coat with red material and wore his hat cocked to one side with a peacock's plume splaying from it. On May 9, 1864, Federal cavalry headed for the Confederate capital to stage a siege of the city. It was during this battle at Yellow Tavern on May 11, 1864, that a Federal trooper fatally wounded General Stuart. He died the following day and was buried in Hollywood Cemetery in Richmond, Va.

*"Major, I am not the same man you were with so long and knew so well. I hope I am a better man now than then. I have been and am trying to lead another kind of life."* – N.B.F.

# General Nathan Bedford Forrest

Born: July 13, 1821, in Chapel Hill, Tennessee
Died: October 29, 1877, in Memphis, Tennessee
Denomination: Presbyterian

Technically, General Nathan Forrest led mounted infantry troops who would dismount to do battle. As a result, the speed with which he could dispatch his soldiers proved to be an invaluable asset and contributed greatly to his many successes. Both feared and revered by his men, Forrest is said to have personally killed thirty troops and had twenty-nine horses shot out from under him in battle. After the war, he bragged that he had come out one horse ahead. Tactically brilliant, Forrest possessed a street-smart approach to battlefield maneuvers, as opposed to the textbook procedures practiced by his opponents from West Point.

BIO: Nathan Forrest was born in Chapel Hill, Tennessee. The oldest child in a poor family of twelve children, he became the head of the household at age seventeen, upon the untimely death of his father. Forrest went on to become a successful businessman, plantation owner and slave trader in Memphis. Though functionally illiterate, he was a self-made millionaire by the time the war broke out in April of 1861. He joined the Confederate States Army and fought with ferocity unequaled on both sides. In his farewell address at the conclusion of the war, Forrest told his troops to be good citizens, as they had been good soldiers. Unfortunately, the corruption of the 'Carpetbaggers,' in taking advantage of the plight of the post-war South, destroyed any chance of the favorable resolution he had promised his men. He became associated with the Ku Klux Klan in an effort to reverse the damage done to the South by these Northerners. In 1867 he was proclaimed the Grand Wizard of the KKK, but resigned his post after serving less than five years. Forrest officially disbanded the Klan's earliest charter in retaliation for the group's violent attacks on the local black citizens. His abandonment of the Klan showed a significant development in his views on race. Faith also played a major role in his transformation. Still, Nathan Bedford Forrest remains one of the most highly debated and controversial figures of the entire Civil War.

*"In the name of God and humanity I protest!"*
– Hood's complaint against Gen. W.T. Sherman's orders to have the citizens of Atlanta leave the city following its capture

# General John Bell Hood

Born: June 1, 1831, in Owingsville, Kentucky
Died: August 30, 1879, in New Orleans, Louisiana
Denomination: Episcopalian

John Hood was the brigade commander of the unit that became known as Hood's "Texas Brigade." At the Battle of Gaines' Mill, he garnered distinction by leading a charge that broke the Union line. Every officer in his brigade was killed or wounded, but Hood remained unscathed. During the infamous Battle of Antietam, Hood's division came to the aid of "Stonewall" Jackson's corps and rescued the Confederate's left flank. Although his performance in the later years of the Civil War left something to be desired, his contributions in some of the Confederacy's greatest victories cannot be denied. Another admirable trait was Hood's fearless admission of faults when defeated. In addition to accepting the blame for tactical failures, he routinely praised his men in after-action reports.

BIO: John B. Hood was the nephew of a U.S. representative named Richard French, who obtained an appointment for him to the U.S. Military Academy. He graduated in 1853, and was ranked 44th in a class of 52 cadets. Upon leaving West Point, he was commissioned as a second lieutenant in the 4th U.S. Infantry and later transferred to the 2nd U.S. Cavalry. Following the attack on Fort Sumter in 1861, Hood resigned his commission in the U. S. Army. Joining the Confederate army, he was quickly promoted to lieutenant colonel. Serving in the Army of Northern Virginia over the next two years, he established himself as a gifted strategist. He saw action at the Seven Days Battles, Second Manassas, Sharpsburg, Fredericksburg and Gettysburg, where he lost the use of an arm. At the bloody Battle of Chickamauga, Hood was severely wounded again, this time losing a leg to amputation. Following his recovery, he was given a corps commander position in the Army of Tennessee and became a key player in the Atlanta Campaign. After the war, he entered the cotton brokerage and insurance businesses in New Orleans. Hood died from yellow fever in 1879, following the death of his wife and child from the same disease. He left behind ten orphaned children.

*He was a devout and humble Christian gentleman. I know of no man more beloved at the South, and he was probably the most popular Southern man among the people of the North.*
– Stephen D. Lee, Commander-in-Chief, U.C.V.

# General John Brown Gordon

Born: February 6, 1832, in Upson County, Georgia
Died: January 9, 1904, in Miami, Florida
Denomination: Episcopalian

General John Gordon was an aggressive commander who was never defeated or repulsed when leading his troops. Assigned by General Robert E. Lee to hold the vital sunken road, or "Bloody Lane," during the Battle of Antietam, he continued to lead his men despite being severely wounded four times. A fifth wound in the face incapacitated him and as a result he was evacuated from the battlefield.

BIO: For more than forty years John B. Gordon was one of the most celebrated citizens of Georgia. He attended the University of Georgia but did not graduate. In 1854 he studied law in Atlanta and by the end of the year passed his bar examination and became a partner in an established law firm. Shortly after the bombardment of Fort Sumter, Gordon helped organize a rebel company of volunteers from Alabama, Georgia and Tennessee. On May 15, 1861, the company mustered into Confederate service as part of the 6th Alabama Infantry. Gen. Gordon's brigade was in the thick of the fighting at Sharpsburg. During this battle he was wounded five times, once in the face. Reportedly, if it had not been for a bullet hole in his hat, he would have drowned in his own blood. His survival is credited to his wife, who nursed her husband back to health. At Appomattox his men made the last charge of the Army of Northern Virginia. After the war, Gordon went on to a distinguished career in politics, serving as a governor and senator, and was active in veterans' affairs. He was generally acknowledged to be the Grand Dragon of the Ku Klux Klan in Georgia, but his role in the organization was never proven conclusively. During the last decade of his life, Gordon remained active in his efforts to vindicate the South, and embarked on a career as an author and lecturer to establish a new spirit of nationalism. He is buried at the Oakland Cemetery in Atlanta, Georgia.

# Photography Index

PUBLIC DOMAIN SOURCES: Library of Congress, Prints & Photographs Division, United States National Archives, National Military Park Service, Notre Dame University Archives, Virginia Military Institute Archives, Museum of the Confederacy Archives, Re-enactor's Missions For Jesus Christ (RMJC), Sons of the South, Sons of Confederate Veterans, and Virginia Commonwealth University.

COVER: Confederate soldiers, Virginia Monument, Gettysburg Battlefield, Pa., Michael Aubrecht. Caption: *Confederate soldiers, Virginia Monument, Gettysburg Battlefield, Pa. (Michael Aubrecht)*

PREFACE: Stained-glass, Trinity Episcopal Church, Natchitoches, La. Caption: *Belltower window depicting Bishop Leonidas Polk (a West Point graduate and Confederate general who was killed at the Battle of Pine Mountain in 1864), commemorating his baptizing of twenty-one slaves in 1853.*

FOREWORD: Artillery position at Devil's Den, Gettysburg Battlefield, Pa., Michael Aubrecht. Caption: *Artillery position at Devil's Den, Gettysburg Battlefield, Pa. (Michael Aubrecht)*

COURAGE: Confederate Artillery, Chancellorsville Battlefield, Va, Michael Aubrecht. Caption: *Confederate Artillery, Chancellorsville Battlefield, Va. (Michael Aubrecht)*

HIS MASTER'S MOUNT: Little Sorrel, Virginia Military Institute Archives. Caption: *Confederate General Thomas "Stonewall" Jackson's mount, Little Sorrel (VMI Archives)*

THE SOUTHERN KNIGHT: Confederate Cavalry General James Ewell Brown (J.E.B.) Stuart, Museum of the Confederacy Archives. Caption: *Confederate Cavalry General James Ewell Brown (J.E.B.) Stuart (MOC Archives)*

LUCK OF THE IRISH: Father William Corby, Notre Dame University Archives. Caption: *Notre Dame University president and Union Army chaplain, Father William Corby (Notre Dame Archives)*

THY WILL BE DONE: Confederate General Thomas "Stonewall" Jackson, Virginia Military Institute Archives. Caption: *Confederate General Thomas "Stonewall" Jackson (VMI Archives)*

PROTESTANT PRESIDENT: Confederate States President Jefferson Davis, Library of Congress, Prints & Photographs Division. Caption: *Confederate States of America President Jefferson Davis (Library of Congress)*

PICKETT'S CHARGE: Confederate General George Pickett, Library of Congress, Prints & Photographs Division. Caption: *Confederate General George Pickett (Library of Congress)*

SAINT AND SINNER: Confederate General Nathan Bedford Forrest, Library of Congress, Prints & Photographs Division. Caption: *Confederate General Nathan Bedford Forrest (Library of Congress)*

DRUMMER BOY: Union Drummer Johnny Clem, United States National Archives. Caption: *Union drummer boy Johnny Clem* (U.S. National Archives)

DUTY: C.S.A. Tennessee Monument, Gettysburg Battlefield, Pa., Michael Aubrecht. Caption: *Tennessee Monument, Gettysburg Battlefield, Pa. (Michael Aubrecht)*

PROVIDENCE IN WAR: 1st Virginia Confederate Militia (Richmond Grays), Library of Congress, Prints & Photographs Division. Caption: *1st Virginia Confederate Militia, Richmond Grays, C.S.A. (Library of Congress)*

CHRISTIAN CAVALIER: Confederate General James Ewell Brown (J.E.B.) Stuart, Museum of the Confederacy Archives. Caption: *Confederate General James Ewell Brown (J.E.B.) Stuart (Museum of the Confederacy Archives)*

THE GOOD SHEPHERD: Jackson marker, Ellwood Plantation, Va., Michael Aubrecht. Caption: *Confederate General Thomas "Stonewall" Jackson's amputated arm marker, Ellwood Manor, Locust Grove, Va. (Michael Aubrecht)*

ROCK OF AGES: Temporary grave marker of Confederate General J.E.B. Stuart, Hollywood Cemetery, Richmond, Va., Library of Congress, Prints & Photographs Division. Caption: *Temporary grave marker of Confederate General J.E.B. Stuart, Hollywood Cemetery, Richmond, Va. (Library of Congress)*

GOD AND GENERAL: Confederate Major General Robert E. Lee, Library of Congress, Prints & Photographs Division. Caption: *Confederate General Robert E. Lee (Library of Congress)*

PLEDGED TO PRAY: Thomas Jonathan Jackson, Virginia Military Institute Archives Caption: *West Point graduate Thomas Jackson, U.S. Army (VMI Archives)*

CHRISTIAN SOLDIERS: C.S.A. Private Edwin Francis Jemison, Library of Congress, Prints & Photographs Division. Caption: *Private Edwin Francis Jemison, 2nd Louisiana Regiment, C.S.A. (Library of Congress)*

CHRISTIAN HERO: Confederate General Robert E. Lee, Library of Congress, Prints & Photographs Division. Caption: *Confederate General Robert E. Lee (Library of Congress)*

FAITH: U.S.A. Irish Brigade Monument, Gettysburg Battlefield, Pa., Michael Aubrecht. Caption: *Union Irish Brigade Monument, Gettysburg Battlefield, Pa. (Michael Aubrecht)*

THE BIBLE BRIGADE: Confederate General Thomas "Stonewall" Jackson, Virginia Military Institute Archives. Caption: *Confederate General Thomas "Stonewall" Jackson (VMI Archives)*

A CHILD'S PASSING: Confederate General James Ewell Brown (J.E.B.) Stuart, Museum of the Confederacy Archives. Caption: *Confederate General James Ewell Brown (J.E.B.) Stuart (MOC Archives)*

THE WIZARD'S WIFE: Confederate General Nathan Bedford Forrest, Library of Congress, Prints & Photographs Division. Caption: *Confederate General Nathan Bedford Forrest (Library of Congress)*

BATTLEFIELD BELIEVER: Union General Oliver Otis Howard, Library of Congress, Prints & Photographs Division. Caption: *Union General Oliver Otis Howard (Library of Congress)*

CONFEDERATE PRAYER: Confederate POWs, Gettysburg, Pa., Library of Congress, Prints & Photographs Division. Caption: *Confederate POWs, Gettysburg, Pa. (Library of Congress)*

STANDING LIKE A STONEWALL: Jackson Monument, Manassas Battlefield, Va., Michael Aubrecht. Caption: *"Stonewall" Jackson Monument, Manassas Battlefield, Va. (Michael Aubrecht)*

CONVERSION IN THE CAMP: Confederate General Richard S. Ewell, Library of Congress, Prints & Photographs Division. Caption: *Confederate General Richard Ewell (Library of Congress)*

BAPTISM UNDER FIRE: U.S. Army Christian Commission Field Headquarters, Library of Congress, Prints & Photographs Division. Caption: *U.S. Army Christian Commission Field Headquarters (Library of Congress)*

HONOR: Unknown Soldier Tombstone, Confederate Cemetery, Spotsylvania, Va., Michael Aubrecht. Caption: *Unknown Soldier, C.S.A. Cemetery, Spotsylvania, Va., (Michael Aubrecht)*

PARENTS AND PRINCIPLES: Confederate Cavalry General James Ewell Brown (J.E.B.) Stuart, Museum of the Confederacy Archives. Caption: *Confederate Cavalry General James Ewell Brown (J.E.B.) Stuart (MOC Archives)*

GAMBLE AT GETTYSBURG: Union casualties, Gettysburg Battlefield, Pa., "The Harvest of Death," Timothy O'Sullivan, Library of Congress, Prints & Photographs Division. Caption: *Union casualties, Gettysburg Battlefield, Pa., (Library of Congress)*

THE PEACEMAKERS: Wilmer McLean house in Appomattox Court House, Va., Library of Congress, Prints & Photographs Division. Caption: *Wilmer McLean house in Appomattox Court House, Va. (Library of Congress)*

PALADIN'S PROSE: Writer, poet, publisher, John Reuben Thompson, United States National Archives. Caption: *Writer, poet, and publisher, John Reuben Thompson (Library of Congress)*

LEE'S CHAPEL: Lee Chapel at Washington College, Va., Washington College. Caption: *Lee Chapel (Washington College)*

THE SOUTHERN CROSS: 10th Mississippi Confederate flag bearer, Silas C. Buck, C.S.A. (Sons of Confederate Veterans). Caption: *10th Mississippi Confederate flag bearer, Silas C. Buck (Sons of Confederate Veterans)*

WIDOW'S WEEDS: Mary Anna Morrison, Virginia Military Institute Archives. Caption: *Confederate General Thomas Jackson's wife Mary Anna Morrison (VMI Archives)*

SONS OF THE SOUTH: Confederate Veterans reunion, Sons of Confederate Veterans Caption: *Confederate Veterans reunion (Sons of Confederate Veterans)*

MERCY: Sgt. Richard Rowland Kirkland Monument, Fredericksburg Battlefield, Va., Michael Aubrecht. Caption: *Kirkland Monument, Fredericksburg Battlefield, Va. (Michael Aubrecht)*

ANGEL OF MARYE'S HEIGHTS: Confederate dead behind the stone wall of Marye's Heights [following the second Battle of Fredericksburg,] Fredericksburg, Va. (National Archives). Caption: *Confederate casualties at the stonewall, Fredericksburg, Va. (National Archives)*

SLAVE SUNDAY SCHOOL: Confederate General Thomas "Stonewall" Jackson, Sons of the South. Caption: *Confederate General Thomas "Stonewall" Jackson (Sons of the South)*

OLD JACK AND LITTLE JANIE: Mary Anna Morrison and daughter Julia Jackson, Virginia Military Institute Archives. Caption: *General Thomas Jackson's widow Mary Anna Morrison and daughter Julia (VMI Archives)*

BLOOD ON THE BATTLEFIELD: Clara Barton, founder of the American Red Cross, Library of Congress, Prints & Photographs Division. Caption: *Clara Barton, founder of the American Red Cross (Library of Congress)*

STONEWALL'S SURGEON: Confederate surgeon Dr. Hunter H. McGuire, M.D., Virginia Commonwealth University. Caption: *Confederate surgeon Dr. Hunter H. McGuire, M.D. (Virginia Commonwealth University)*

MOTHERS OF MERCY: Wounded from the Battle of the Wilderness, Va., Library of Congress, Prints & Photographs Division. Caption: *Wounded from the Battle of the Wilderness, Va. (Library of Congress)*

SOUTHERN SPY: Confederate spy Ms. Emeline Pigott, National Archives. Caption: *Confederate spy Ms. Emeline Pigott (National Archives)*

TRUST IN HIM: Confederate infantry private and Union cavalry trooper, Library of Congress, Prints & Photographs Division. Caption: *Brother against brother, a Confederate infantry private and Union cavalry trooper (Library of Congress)*

ESSAYS OF ENCOURAGEMENT: Artillery position at Devil's Den, Gettysburg Battlefield, Pa., Michael Aubrecht. Caption: *Artillery position at Devil's Den, Gettysburg Battlefield, Pa. (Michael Aubrecht)*

THE SOUTHERN SAMARITAN: Sgt. Kirkland Monument, Fredericksburg Battlefield, Va., Michael Aubrecht. Caption: *Kirkland Monument, Fredericksburg Battlefield, Va. (Michael Aubrecht)*
EPILOGUE: Kirkland portrait, Library of Congress, Prints & Photographs Division.

PATERNAL PROMISE: Confederate General Thomas "Stonewall" Jackson position marker, Fredericksburg, Va., Michael Aubrecht. Caption: *Confederate General Thomas "Stonewall" Jackson field marker, Fredericksburg, Va. (Michael Aubrecht)*

THE BIBLE BRIGADE: Lt. Bartley Pace Bynum, C.S.A., also chaplain in the Confederate Army, Library of Congress, Prints & Photographs Division. Caption: *Confederate Chaplain Lt. Bartley Pace Bynum (Library of Congress)*

PEACE BE WITH YOU: Union General Ulysses S. Grant, Library of Congress, Prints & Photographs Division. Caption: *Union General Ulysses S. Grant (Library of Congress)*

THE FIGHTING IRISH: Father William Corby Monument, Gettysburg Battlefield, Pa., Michael Aubrecht. Caption: *Father Corby Monument, Gettysburg Battlefield, Pa. (Michael Aubrecht)*

CHAPLAINS IN THE CONFEDERACY: Confederate veteran, Sons of Confederate Veterans. Caption: *Confederate veteran (Sons of Confederate Veterans)*

STONEWALL'S STEED: Little Sorrel on campus grounds at Virginia Military Institute, Virginia Military Institute Archives. Caption: *Confederate General Thomas "Stonewall" Jackson's mount Little Sorrel on campus grounds at Virginia Military Institute (VMI Archives)*

THE CHRISTIAN GENERAL: Union General Oliver Otis Howard, Library of Congress, Prints & Photographs Division. Caption: *Union general and founder of Howard University Oliver Howard (Library of Congress)*

STONEWALL'S SABBATH SCHOOL: Contrabands originally from Virginia, Library of Congress, Prints & Photographs Division. Caption: *Group of contrabands (Library of Congress)*

GUIDANCE AND GRACE: Confederate General James Ewell Brown Stuart, Museum of the Confederacy Archives. Caption: *General James Ewell Brown (J.E.B.) Stuart (MOC Archives)*

WALT WHITMAN, ABRAHAM LINCOLN, PAMUNKEY RIVER CAMP: Mathew Brady Studio. Courtesy of United States Library of Congress. Caption *Portraits of Poet Walt Whitman, President Abraham Lincoln. Federal troops overlooking their camp near the Pamunkey River in Virginia.*

# Illustration Index

SERMON: Christ in the Camp illustration, Library of Congress, Prints & Photographs Division. Caption: *Period illustration depicting church service in a Confederate camp (Library of Congress)*

RELIGION IN THE RANKS: Typeset cover of Confederate devotional book, RMJC.
Caption: *Pocket prayer book, printed in Charleston and distributed to troops on the march (RMJC Archives)*

BATTLE AT WILLIS CHURCH: Frank Leslie, *Famous Leaders and Battle Scenes of the Civil War* (New York: Mrs. Frank Leslie, 1896)

GEN. ROBERT E. LEE: Wilbur F. Gody, *A History of the US for Schools* (N.Y.: Charles Scribner's Sons, 1916)

GEN. THOMAS J. JACKSON: Wilbur F. Gody, *A History of the US for Schools* (N.Y.: Charles Scribner's Sons, 1916)

GEN. JEB STUART: Chandler B. Beach, *The New Student's Reference Work for Teachers Students and Families* (Chicago: F. E. Compton and Company, 1909)

GEN. NATHAN B. FORREST: Chandler B. Beach, *The New Student's Reference Work for Teachers Students and Families* (Chicago: F. E. Compton and Company, 1909)

GEN. JOHN BELL HOOD: Chandler B. Beach, *The New Student's Reference Work for Teachers Students and Families* (Chicago: F. E. Compton and Company, 1909)

GEN. JOHN B. GORDON: Chandler B. Beach, *The New Student's Reference Work for Teachers Students and Families* (Chicago: F. E. Compton and Company, 1909)

# Bibliography

PRINT MEDIA:

Aubrecht, Michael. *Onward Christian Soldier: The Spiritual Journey of Stonewall.* Publish America 2005. *Christian Cavalier: The Spiritual Journey of J.E.B. Stuart.* Publish America 2005.

Berggren, Jason D. *Jefferson Davis, Religion and the Politics of Recognition.* Journal Title: White House Studies. Volume: 5. Issue: 2. 2005.

Corby, William. *Memoirs of Chaplain Life: Three Years with the Irish Brigade in the Army of the Potomac.* Scholastic Press, 1894.

Coski, John M. *The Confederate Battle Flag: America's Most Embattled Emblem.* Belknap Press; Reprint edition, 2006.

Dabney, Robert Lewis. *Life and Campaigns of Lieut. Gen. Thomas J. Jackson, (Stonewall Jackson).* Sprinkle Publications, 1983.

Davis, Burke. *J.E.B. Stuart: The Last Cavalier.* New York: Rinehart & Co., Inc. 1957.

Jones, William J. *Christ In The Camp.* The Vision Forum, Inc., 1999.

Henderson, G.F.R. *Stonewall Jackson and the American Civil War.* Cambridge, MA: Da Capo Press, 1998.

Hurst, Jack. *Nathan Bedford Forrest: A Biography.* Vintage; Reprint edition, 1994.

Lee, Robert E. *The Recollections & Letters of Robert E. Lee.* Smithmark Publishers; Reprint, 1998.

McGuire, Dr. Hunter, Chief Surgeon of the Second Corps. *Reminiscences of the Famous Leader.*

Morrison, Mary Anna. *Life and Letters of General Thomas J. Jackson by his Wife Mary Anna Jackson.* New York, NY. Harper, 1892.

Pfanz, Donald C. *Richard S. Ewell: A Soldier's Life.* UNC Press, 1998.

Robertson, James I. *Stonewall Jackson: The Man, the Soldier and the Legend.* New York, NY: MacMillan Publishing Company, 1997.

Shattuck, Dr. Gardiner H. Jr. *A Shield and Hiding Place: The Religious Life of the Civil War Armies.* Mercer University Press, 1987.

Studdard, Kenneth. *Is That Enough? The Life Of General Nathan Bedford Forrest.* Sermon transcript, January 26, 1997. Pleasant Grove Baptist Church. Summerville, Georgia.

Thompson, John Reuben. *Obsequies of Stuart. (May 12, 1864).* Richmond, Va.: Virginia Historical Society.

Verses. Scripture passages are taken from the *Holy Bible, King James Version®*. Copyright © 1973, 1978, 1984 International Bible Society.

Williams, Richard G. Jr. and James. I. Robertson Jr. *Stonewall Jackson: The Black Man's Friend.* Cumberland House Publishing, 2006.

DIGITAL MEDIA:

*Civil War Nurses: The Angels of the Battlefield.* Home of the American Civil War, 2003.

*For God and Country: The Role of Religion in the Civil War.* M. Aubrecht/Pinstripe Press, 2006.

*Gods and Generals: Life of Stonewall Jackson.* Bonus Feature. Directed by Ronald F. Maxwell. Warner Home Video, 2003. DVD Edition.

*The Battle Rainbow: Jackson and his Chaplains* by Russ Campbell. Military History Online, 2003.

PERMISSIONS:

"Death of Stonewall Jackson." Southern Historical Society Papers, Vol. XIV. Richmond, Va. January-December, 1886. Courtesy of Southern Historical Society and *AmericanCivilWar.com.*

"The Real Stonewall Jackson." Interview with General Daniel H. Hill. *Century Magazine,* February, 1894. Courtesy of Brad Haugaard.

"Stonewall Jackson, the Consummate Prayer-Warrior of Romans 8:28." Accounts by Reverend Dr. William S. White of the Lexington Presbyterian Church. 1888. Courtesy of Christian Heritage Library.

Thomas Jackson obituary transcript. Printed in *Harper's Weekly*, May 30, 1863. Courtesy of Sons of the South.

Thomas Jackson postmortem tribute. *Richmond Times Dispatch.* May, 1863. Courtesy of the *Richmond Times Dispatch.*

"Death of J.E.B. Stuart." *Southern Historical Society Papers*, Vol. VII, No. 2. Richmond, Va. February, 1879. Courtesy of Southern Historical Society and *AmericanCivilWar.com.*

"Notification of Mrs. Stuart." *Southern Historical Society Papers*, Vol. VII, No. 3. Richmond, Va. March, 1879. Courtesy of Southern Historical Society and *AmericanCivilWar.com.*

"General Stuart's Wounding at Yellow Tavern and his Subsequent Death in Richmond." *Southern Historical Society Papers*, Vol. XXVI. Richmond, Va. January–December, 1898. Courtesy of Southern Historical Society and *AmericanCivilWar.com.*

"Major H. B. McClellan and Captain R. E. Frayser's Tribute to J.E.B. Stuart." *Southern Historical Society Papers*, Vol. XXX. Richmond, Va. January–December, 1902. Courtesy of Southern Historical Society and *AmericanCivilWar.com.*

J.E.B. Stuart obituary transcript. Printed in *Harper's Weekly*, August 6, 1864. Courtesy of Sons of the South.

# About The Authors

MICHAEL AUBRECHT has dedicated his studies to the role of Christianity during the Civil War. He is the author of numerous articles and books on the subject including *Onward Christian Soldier: The Spiritual Journey of Stonewall, Christian Cavalier: The Spiritual Legacy of JEB Stuart* and *Houses of the Holy: Historic Churches of Fredericksburg*. From 2000-2006, Michael authored over 375 separate studies on the history of America's national pastime for *Baseball-Almanac,* as well as the eBook *Luckiest Fans On The Face Of This Earth: The History of New York Yankees Fall Classics.* In 2004, Michael joined the online authors group, Faith Writers, and began writing Christian material that has been published in multiple religious magazines and periodicals. He has also been active as a contributing writer for the *Spotsylvania Presbyterian Church Post* since 2003. In late 2004 and again in early 2005, Michael published his first two books focusing on the Christian character of Confederate generals. Two more releases followed in 2008. Today, Michael writes historical features and book reviews for *The Free Lance-Star* newspaper and *Civil War Historian* magazine. Michael is also a founding member of the Jackson Society, an Associate Member of the Sons of Confederate Veterans (Camp #1296), an Honorary Member of the John Bell Hood Historical Society, and a proud supporter of the Gettysburg Foundation. A popular speaker, Michael has presented custom lectures to heritage groups, church organizations, round tables and universities. He currently resides in historic Fredericksburg, Virginia with his wife and four children. The Aubrecht family attends Spotsylvania Presbyterian Church. For more information, visit Michael's website and blog at www.pinstripepress.net.

Also by Michael Aubrecht:
*Onward Christian Soldier: The Spiritual Journey of Stonewall*
*Christian Cavalier: The Spiritual Legacy of J.E.B. Stuart*
*Houses of the Holy: Historic Churches of Fredericksburg*

RICHARD G. WILLIAMS, JR. is an award-winning author and frequent speaker on subjects related to the Civil War. A regular contributor to the *Washington Time's* Civil War column, he has also written for *Homeschooling Today Magazine* and regularly contributes articles about the War Between the States to newspapers and other publications. He has spoken at Liberty University's Annual Civil War Seminar at Lee Chapel in Lexington, Virginia, West Virginia University's Jackson's Mill and other history related functions as well. He co-produced the video series, *Institute on the Constitution* with constitutional attorney John Eidsmoe. The production won a national award from the Freedoms Foundation at Valley Forge. His passion for America's Christian history has led him to author three books: *Christian Business Legends, The Maxims of Robert E. Lee for Young Gentlemen* and *Stonewall Jackson: The Black Man's Friend.* His latest book is the basis for a new documentary by Franklin Springs Family Media titled *Still Standing: The Stonewall Jackson Story.* Williams has worked as a publisher, producer, free-lance writer, book reviewer, documentary film consultant and a magistrate for the Commonwealth of Virginia. He lives with his wife and children in Virginia's Shenandoah Valley. For more information, visit Richard's website and blog at www.southriverbooks.com.

Also by Richard Williams:
*The Maxims of Robert E. Lee for Young Gentlemen*
*Stonewall Jackson: The Black Man's Friend*
*Christian Business Legends*

# Daily Bread For The Prayer Warrior

*It only takes about 30 minutes a day to read the entire bible in one year using this schedule.*

Among Thomas "Stonewall" Jackson's many favorite bible verses was the Fifth Chapter of Second Corinthians, which was recorded as the last scripture that he shared with his wife before going off to serve his God and country. It states, "For we know that if the earthly house of this tabernacle were dissolved, we have a building of God, a house not made with hands, eternal in the heavens." While on campaign, Jackson maintained his obedient study schedule to the best of his ability and remained a steadfast prayer warrior who began every day, at the first sign of dawn, strengthening his faith and pledging that Jesus Christ alone was his Savior. Even today many of us can draw some inspiration from the general's example. If the study of scripture can give one man the "spiritual armor" required to stand, unflinching on a battlefield, dealing with the daily rigors of wartime existence while maintaining a strong faith in God, imagine what a positive and powerful influence it can be in your life.

## January

| | | | |
|---|---|---|---|
| 1 | Luke 5:27-39 | Genesis 1-2 | Psalm 1 |
| 2 | Luke 6:1-26 | Genesis 3-5 | Psalm 2 |
| 3 | Luke 6:27-49 | Genesis 6-7 | Psalm 3 |
| 4 | Luke 7:1-17 | Genesis 8-10 | Psalm 4 |
| 5 | Luke 7:18-50 | Genesis 11 | Psalm 5 |
| 6 | Luke 8:1-25 | Genesis 12 | Psalm 6 |
| 7 | Luke 8:26-56 | Genesis 13-14 | Psalm 7 |
| 8 | Luke 9:1-27 | Genesis 15 | Psalm 8 |
| 9 | Luke 9:28-62 | Genesis 16 | Psalm 9 |
| 10 | Luke 10:1-20 | Genesis 17 | Psalm 10 |
| 11 | Luke 10:21-42 | Genesis 18 | Psalm 11 |
| 12 | Luke 11:1-28 | Genesis 19 | Psalm 12 |
| 13 | Luke 11:29-54 | Genesis 20 | Psalm 13 |
| 14 | Luke 12:1-31 | Genesis 21 | Psalm 14 |
| 15 | Luke 12:32-59 | Genesis 22 | Psalm 15 |
| 16 | Luke 13:1-17 | Genesis 23 | Psalm 16 |
| 17 | Luke 13:18-35 | Genesis 24 | Psalm 17 |

| | | | |
|---|---|---|---|
| 18 | Luke 14:1-24 | Genesis 25 | Psalm 18 |
| 19 | Luke 14:25-35 | Genesis 26 | Psalm 19 |
| 20 | Luke 15 | Genesis 27:1-45 | Psalm 20 |
| 21 | Luke 16 | Genesis 27:46-28:22 | Psalm 21 |
| 22 | Luke 17 | Genesis 29:1-30 | Psalm 22 |
| 23 | Luke 18:1-17 | Genesis 29:31-30:43 | Psalm 23 |
| 24 | Luke 18:18-43 | Genesis 31 | Psalm 24 |
| 25 | Luke 19:1-27 | Genesis 32-33 | Psalm 25 |
| 26 | Luke 19:28-48 | Genesis 34 | Psalm 26 |
| 27 | Luke 20:1-26 | Genesis 35-36 | Psalm 27 |
| 28 | Luke 20:27-47 | Genesis 37 | Psalm 28 |
| 29 | Luke 21 | Genesis 38 | Psalm 29 |
| 30 | Luke 22:1-38 | Genesis 39 | Psalm 30 |
| 31 | Luke 22:39-71 | Genesis 40 | Psalm 31 |

## February

| | | | |
|---|---|---|---|
| 1 | Luke 23:1-25 | Genesis 41 | Psalm 32 |
| 2 | Luke 23:26-56 | Genesis 42 | Psalm 33 |
| 3 | Luke 24:1-12 | Genesis 43 | Psalm 34 |
| 4 | Luke 24:13-53 | Genesis 44 | Psalm 35 |
| 5 | Hebrews 1 | Genesis 45:1-46:27 | Psalm 36 |
| 6 | Hebrews 2 | Genesis 46:28-47:31 | Psalm 37 |
| 7 | Hebrews 3:1-4:13 | Genesis 48 | Psalm 38 |
| 8 | Hebrews 4:14-6:12 | Genesis 49-50 | Psalm 39 |
| 9 | Hebrews 6:13-20 | Exodus 1-2 | Psalm 40 |
| 10 | Hebrews 7 | Exodus 3-4 | Psalm 41 |
| 11 | Hebrews 8 | Exodus 5:1-6:27 | Proverbs 1 |
| 12 | Hebrews 9:1-22 | Exodus 6:28-8:32 | Proverbs 2 |
| 13 | Hebrews 9:23-10:18 | Exodus 9-10 | Proverbs 3 |
| 14 | Hebrews 10:19-39 | Exodus 11-12 | Proverbs 4 |
| 15 | Hebrews 11:1-22 | Exodus 13-14 | Proverbs 5 |
| 16 | Hebrews 11:23-40 | Exodus 15 | Proverbs 6:1-7:5 |
| 17 | Hebrews 12 | Exodus 16-17 | Proverbs 7:6-27 |
| 18 | Hebrews 13 | Exodus 18-19 | Proverbs 8 |
| 19 | Matthew 1 | Exodus 20-21 | Proverbs 9 |
| 20 | Matthew 2 | Exodus 22-23 | Proverbs 10 |
| 21 | Matthew 3 | Exodus 24 | Proverbs 11 |
| 22 | Matthew 4 | Exodus 25-27 | Proverbs 12 |
| 23 | Matthew 5:1-20 | Exodus 28-29 | Proverbs 13 |
| 24 | Matthew 5:21-48 | Exodus 30-32 | Proverbs 14 |
| 25 | Matthew 6:1-18 | Exodus 33-34 | Proverbs 15 |
| 26 | Matthew 6:19-34 | Exodus 35-36 | Proverbs 16 |
| 27 | Matthew 7 | Exodus 37-38 | Proverbs 17 |
| 28 | Matthew 8:1-13 | Exodus 39-40 | Proverbs 18 |

## March

| | | | |
|---|---|---|---|
| 1 | Matthew 8:14-34 | Leviticus 1-2 | Proverbs 19 |
| 2 | Matthew 9:1-17 | Leviticus 3-4 | Proverbs 20 |
| 3 | Matthew 9:18-38 | Leviticus 5-6 | Proverbs 21 |
| 4 | Matthew 10:1-25 | Leviticus 7-8 | Proverbs 22 |
| 5 | Matthew 10:26-42 | Leviticus 9-10 | Proverbs 23 |
| 6 | Matthew 11:1-19 | Leviticus 11-12 | Proverbs 24 |
| 7 | Matthew 11:20-30 | Leviticus 13 | Proverbs 25 |
| 8 | Matthew 12:1-21 | Leviticus 14 | Proverbs 26 |
| 9 | Matthew 12:22-50 | Leviticus 15-16 | Proverbs 27 |
| 10 | Matthew 13:1-23 | Leviticus 17-18 | Proverbs 28 |
| 11 | Matthew 13:24-58 | Leviticus 19 | Proverbs 29 |
| 12 | Matthew 14:1-21 | Leviticus 20-21 | Proverbs 30 |
| 13 | Matthew 14:22-36 | Leviticus 22-23 | Proverbs 31 |
| 14 | Matthew 15:1-20 | Leviticus 24-25 | Ecclesiastes 1:1-11 |
| 15 | Matthew 15:21-39 | Leviticus 26-27 | Ecclesiastes 1:12-2:26 |
| 16 | Matthew 16 | Numbers 1-2 | Ecclesiastes 3:1-15 |
| 17 | Matthew 17 | Numbers 3-4 | Ecclesiastes 3:16-4:16 |
| 18 | Matthew 18:1-20 | Numbers 5-6 | Ecclesiastes 5 |
| 19 | Matthew 18:21-35 | Numbers 7-8 | Ecclesiastes 6 |
| 20 | Matthew 19:1-15 | Numbers 9-10 | Ecclesiastes 7 |
| 21 | Matthew 19:16-30 | Numbers 11-12 | Ecclesiastes 8 |
| 22 | Matthew 20:1-16 | Numbers 13-14 | Ecclesiastes 9:1-12 |
| 23 | Matthew 20:17-34 | Numbers 15-16 | Ecclesiastes 9:13-10:20 |
| 24 | Matthew 21:1-27 | Numbers 17-18 | Ecclesiastes 11:1-8 |
| 25 | Matthew 21:28-46 | Numbers 19-20 | Ecclesiastes 11:9-12:14 |
| 26 | Matthew 22:1-22 | Numbers 21 | Song of Solomon 1:1-2:7 |
| 27 | Matthew 22:23-46 | Numbers 22:1-40 | Song of Solomon 2:8-3:5 |
| 28 | Matthew 23:1-12 | Numbers 22:41-23:26 | Song of Solomon 3:6-5:1 |
| 29 | Matthew 23:13-39 | Numbers 23:27-24:25 | Song of Solomon 5:2-6:3 |
| 30 | Matthew 24:1-31 | Numbers 25-27 | Song of Solomon 6:4-8:4 |
| 31 | Matthew 24:32-51 | Numbers 28-29 | Song of Solomon 8:5-14 |

## April

| | | | |
|---|---|---|---|
| 1 | Matthew 25:1-30 | Numbers 30-31 | Job 1 |
| 2 | Matthew 25:31-46 | Numbers 32-34 | Job 2 |
| 3 | Matthew 26:1-25 | Numbers 35-36 | Job 3 |
| 4 | Matthew 26:26-46 | Deuteronomy 1-2 | Job 4 |
| 5 | Matthew 26:47-75 | Deuteronomy 3-4 | Job 5 |
| 6 | Matthew 27:1-31 | Deuteronomy 5-6 | Job 6 |
| 7 | Matthew 27:32-66 | Deuteronomy 7-8 | Job 7 |
| 8 | Matthew 28 | Deuteronomy 9-10 | Job 8 |
| 9 | Acts 1 | Deuteronomy 11-12 | Job 9 |

| | | | |
|---|---|---|---|
| 10 | Acts 2:1-13 | Deuteronomy 13-14 | Job 10 |
| 11 | Acts 2:14-47 | Deuteronomy 15-16 | Job 11 |
| 12 | Acts 3 | Deuteronomy 17-18 | Job 12 |
| 13 | Acts 4:1-22 | Deuteronomy 19-20 | Job 13 |
| 14 | Acts 4:23-37 | Deuteronomy 21-22 | Job 14 |
| 15 | Acts 5:1-16 | Deuteronomy 23-24 | Job 15 |
| 16 | Acts 5:17-42 | Deuteronomy 25-27 | Job 16 |
| 17 | Acts 6 | Deuteronomy 28 | Job 17 |
| 18 | Acts 7:1-22 | Deuteronomy 29-30 | Job 18 |
| 19 | Acts 7:23-8:1 | Deuteronomy 31-32 | Job 19 |
| 20 | Acts 8:1-25 | Deuteronomy 33-34 | Job 20 |
| 21 | Acts 8:26-40 | Joshua 1-2 | Job 21 |
| 22 | Acts 9:1-25 | Joshua 3:1-5:1 | Job 22 |
| 23 | Acts 9:26-43 | Joshua 5:2-6:27 | Job 23 |
| 24 | Acts 10:1-33 | Joshua 7-8 | Job 24 |
| 25 | Acts 10:34-48 | Joshua 9-10 | Job 25 |
| 26 | Acts 11:1-18 | Joshua 11-12 | Job 26 |
| 27 | Acts 11:19-30 | Joshua 13-14 | Job 27 |
| 28 | Acts 12 | Joshua 15-17 | Job 28 |
| 29 | Acts 13:1-25 | Joshua 18-19 | Job 29 |
| 30 | Acts 13:26-52 | Joshua 20-21 | Job 30 |

May

| | | | |
|---|---|---|---|
| 1 | Acts 14 | Joshua 22 | Job 31 |
| 2 | Acts 15:1-21 | Joshua 23-24 | Job 32 |
| 3 | Acts 15:22-41 | Judges 1 | Job 33 |
| 4 | Acts 16:1-15 | Judges 2-3 | Job 34 |
| 5 | Acts 16:16-40 | Judges 4-5 | Job 35 |
| 6 | Acts 17:1-15 | Judges 6 | Job 36 |
| 7 | Acts 17:16-34 | Judges 7-8 | Job 37 |
| 8 | Acts 18 | Judges 9 | Job 38 |
| 9 | Acts 19:1-20 | Judges 10:1-11:33 | Job 39 |
| 10 | Acts 19:21-41 | Judges 11:34-12:15 | Job 40 |
| 11 | Acts 20:1-16 | Judges 13 | Job 41 |
| 12 | Acts 20:17-38 | Judges 14-15 | Job 42 |
| 13 | Acts 21:1-36 | Judges 16 | Psalm 42 |
| 14 | Acts 21:37-22:29 | Judges 17-18 | Psalm 43 |
| 15 | Acts 22:30-23:22 | Judges 19 | Psalm 44 |
| 16 | Acts 23:23-24:9 | Judges 20 | Psalm 45 |
| 17 | Acts 24:10-27 | Judges 21 | Psalm 46 |
| 18 | Acts 25 | Ruth 1-2 | Psalm 47 |
| 19 | Acts 26:1-18 | Ruth 3-4 | Psalm 48 |
| 20 | Acts 26:19-32 | 1 Samuel 1:1-2:10 | Psalm 49 |
| 21 | Acts 27:1-12 | 1 Samuel 2:11-36 | Psalm 50 |

| | | | |
|---|---|---|---|
| 22 | Acts 27:13-44 | 1 Samuel 3 | Psalm 51 |
| 23 | Acts 28:1-16 | 1 Samuel 4-5 | Psalm 52 |
| 24 | Acts 28:17-31 | 1 Samuel 6-7 | Psalm 53 |
| 25 | Romans 1:1-15 | 1 Samuel 8 | Psalm 54 |
| 26 | Romans 1:16-32 | 1 Samuel 9:1-10:16 | Psalm 55 |
| 27 | Romans 2:1-3:8 | 1 Samuel 10:17-11:15 | Psalm 56 |
| 28 | Romans 3:9-31 | 1 Samuel 12 | Psalm 57 |
| 29 | Romans 4 | 1 Samuel 13 | Psalm 58 |
| 30 | Romans 5 | 1 Samuel 14 | Psalm 59 |
| 31 | Romans 6 | 1 Samuel 15 | Psalm 60 |

## June

| | | | |
|---|---|---|---|
| 1 | Romans 7 | 1 Samuel 16 | Psalm 61 |
| 2 | Romans 8 | 1 Samuel 17:1-54 | Psalm 62 |
| 3 | Romans 9:1-29 | 1 Samuel 17:55-18:30 | Psalm 63 |
| 4 | Romans 9:30-10:21 | 1 Samuel 19 | Psalm 64 |
| 5 | Romans 11:1-24 | 1 Samuel 20 | Psalm 65 |
| 6 | Romans 11:25-36 | 1 Samuel 21-22 | Psalm 66 |
| 7 | Romans 12 | 1 Samuel 23-24 | Psalm 67 |
| 8 | Romans 13 | 1 Samuel 25 | Psalm 68 |
| 9 | Romans 14 | 1 Samuel 26 | Psalm 69 |
| 10 | Romans 15:1-13 | 1 Samuel 27-28 | Psalm 70 |
| 11 | Romans 15:14-33 | 1 Samuel 29-31 | Psalm 71 |
| 12 | Romans 16 | 2 Samuel 1 | Psalm 72 |
| 13 | Mark 1:1-20 | 2 Samuel 2:1-3:1 | Daniel 1 |
| 14 | Mark 1:21-45 | 2 Samuel 3:2-39 | Daniel 2:1-23 |
| 15 | Mark 2 | 2 Samuel 4-5 | Daniel 2:24-49 |
| 16 | Mark 3:1-19 | 2 Samuel 6 | Daniel 3 |
| 17 | Mark 3:20-35 | 2 Samuel 7-8 | Daniel 4 |
| 18 | Mark 4:1-20 | 2 Samuel 9-10 | Daniel 5 |
| 19 | Mark 4:21-41 | 2 Samuel 11-12 | Daniel 6 |
| 20 | Mark 5:1-20 | 2 Samuel 13 | Daniel 7 |
| 21 | Mark 5:21-43 | 2 Samuel 14 | Daniel 8 |
| 22 | Mark 6:1-29 | 2 Samuel 15 | Daniel 9 |
| 23 | Mark 6:30-56 | 2 Samuel 16 | Daniel 10:1-21 |
| 24 | Mark 7:1-13 | 2 Samuel 17 | Daniel 11:1-19 |
| 25 | Mark 7:14-37 | 2 Samuel 18 | Daniel 11:20-45 |
| 26 | Mark 8:1-21 | 2 Samuel 19 | Daniel 12 |
| 27 | Mark 8:22-9:1 | 2 Samuel 20-21 | Hosea 1:1-2:1 |
| 28 | Mark 9:2-50 | 2 Samuel 22 | Hosea 2:2-23 |
| 29 | Mark 10:1-31 | 2 Samuel 23 | Hosea 3 |
| 30 | Mark 10:32-52 | 2 Samuel 24 | Hosea 4:1-11 |

## July

| | | | |
|---|---|---|---|
| 1 | Mark 11:1-14 | 1 Kings 1 | Hosea 4:1-5:4 |
| 2 | Mark 11:15-33 | 1 Kings 2 | Hosea 5:5-15 |
| 3 | Mark 12:1-27 | 1 Kings 3 | Hosea 6:1-7:2 |
| 4 | Mark 12:28-44 | 1 Kings 4-5 | Hosea 7:3-16 |
| 5 | Mark 13:1-13 | 1 Kings 6 | Hosea 8 |
| 6 | Mark 13:14-37 | 1 Kings 7 | Hosea 9:1-16 |
| 7 | Mark 14:1-31 | 1 Kings 8 | Hosea 9:17-10:15 |
| 8 | Mark 14:32-72 | 1 Kings 9 | Hosea 11:1-11 |
| 9 | Mark 15:1-20 | 1 Kings 10 | Hosea 11:12-12:14 |
| 10 | Mark 15:21-47 | 1 Kings 11 | Hosea 13 |
| 11 | Mark 16 | 1 Kings 12:1-31 | Hosea 14 |
| 12 | 1 Corinthians 1:1-17 | 1 Kings 12:32-13:34 | Joel 1 |
| 13 | 1 Corinthians 1:18-31 | 1 Kings 14 | Joel 2:1-11 |
| 14 | 1 Corinthians 2 | 1 Kings 15:1-32 | Joel 2:12-32 |
| 15 | 1 Corinthians 3 | 1 Kings 15:33-16:34 | Joel 3 |
| 16 | 1 Corinthians 4 | 1 Kings 17 | Amos 1 |
| 17 | 1 Corinthians 5 | 1 Kings 18 | Amos 2:1-3:2 |
| 18 | 1 Corinthians 6 | 1 Kings 19 | Amos 3:3-4:3 |
| 19 | 1 Corinthians 7:1-24 | 1 Kings 20 | Amos 4:4-13 |
| 20 | 1 Corinthians 7:25-40 | 1 Kings 21 | Amos 5 |
| 21 | 1 Corinthians 8 | 1 Kings 22 | Amos 6 |
| 22 | 1 Corinthians 9 | 2 Kings 1-2 | Amos 7 |
| 23 | 1 Corinthians 10 | 2 Kings 3 | Amos 8 |
| 24 | 1 Corinthians 11:1-16 | 2 Kings 4 | Amos 9 |
| 25 | 1 Corinthians 11:17-34 | 2 Kings 5 | Obadiah 1 |
| 26 | 1 Corinthians 12 | 2 Kings 6:1-7:2 | Jonah 1 |
| 27 | 1 Corinthians 13 | 2 Kings 7:3-20 | Jonah 2 |
| 28 | 1 Corinthians 14:1-25 | 2 Kings 8 | Jonah 3 |
| 29 | 1 Corinthians 14:26-40 | 2 Kings 9 | Jonah 4 |
| 30 | 1 Corinthians 15:1-34 | 2 Kings 10 | Micah 1 |
| 31 | 1 Corinthians 15:35-58 | 2 Kings 11 | Micah 2 |

## August

| | | | |
|---|---|---|---|
| 1 | 1 Corinthians 16 | 2 Kings 12-13 | Micah 3 |
| 2 | 2 Corinthians 1:1-2:4 | 2 Kings 14 | Micah 4:1-5:1 |
| 3 | 2 Corinthians 2:5-3:18 | 2 Kings 15-16 | Micah 5:2-15 |
| 4 | 2 Corinthians 4:1-5:10 | 2 Kings 17 | Micah 6 |
| 5 | 2 Corinthians 5:11-6:13 | 2 Kings 18 | Micah 7 |
| 6 | 2 Corinthians 6:14-7:16 | 2 Kings 19 | Nahum 1 |
| 7 | 2 Corinthians 8 | 2 Kings 20-21 | Nahum 2 |
| 8 | 2 Corinthians 9 | 2 Kings 22:1-23:35 | Nahum 3 |
| 9 | 2 Corinthians 10 | 2 Kings 23:36-24:20 | Habakkuk 1 |

| | | | |
|---|---|---|---|
| 10 | 2 Corinthians 11 | 2 Kings 25 | Habakkuk 2 |
| 11 | 2 Corinthians 12 | 1 Chronicles 1-2 | Habakkuk 3 |
| 12 | 2 Corinthians 13 | 1 Chronicles 3-4 | Zephaniah 1 |
| 13 | John 1:1-18 | 1 Chronicles 5-6 | Zephaniah 2 |
| 14 | John 1:19-34 | 1 Chronicles 7-8 | Zephaniah 3 |
| 15 | John 1:35-51 | 1 Chronicles 9 | Haggai 1-2 |
| 16 | John 2 | 1 Chronicles 10-11 | Zechariah 1 |
| 17 | John 3:1-21 | 1 Chronicles 12 | Zechariah 2 |
| 18 | John 3:22-36 | 1 Chronicles 13-14 | Zechariah 3 |
| 19 | John 4:1-26 | 1 Chronicles 15:1-16:6 | Zechariah 4 |
| 20 | John 4:27-42 | 1 Chronicles 16:7-43 | Zechariah 5 |
| 21 | John 4:43-54 | 1 Chronicles 17 | Zechariah 6 |
| 22 | John 5:1-18 | 1 Chronicles 18-19 | Zechariah 7 |
| 23 | John 5:19-47 | 1 Chronicles 20:1-22:1 | Zechariah 8 |
| 24 | John 6:1-21 | 1 Chronicles 22:2-23:32 | Zechariah 9 |
| 25 | John 6:22-59 | 1 Chronicles 24 | Zechariah 10 |
| 26 | John 6:60-71 | 1 Chronicles 25-26 | Zechariah 11 |
| 27 | John 7:1-24 | 1 Chronicles 27-28 | Zechariah 12 |
| 28 | John 7:25-52 | 1 Chronicles 29 | Zechariah 13 |
| 29 | John 8:1-20 | 2 Chronicles 1:1-2:16 | Zechariah 14 |
| 30 | John 8:21-47 | 2 Chronicles 2:17-5:1 | Malachi 1:1-2:9 |
| 31 | John 8:48-59 | 2 Chronicles 5:2-14 | Malachi 2:10-16 |

## September

| | | | |
|---|---|---|---|
| 1 | John 9:1-23 | 2 Chronicles 6 | Malachi 2:17-3:18 |
| 2 | John 9:24-41 | 2 Chronicles 7 | Malachi 4 |
| 3 | John 10:1-21 | 2 Chronicles 8 | Psalm 73 |
| 4 | John 10:22-42 | 2 Chronicles 9 | Psalm 74 |
| 5 | John 11:1-27 | 2 Chronicles 10-11 | Psalm 75 |
| 6 | John 11:28-57 | 2 Chronicles 12-13 | Psalm 76 |
| 7 | John 12:1-26 | 2 Chronicles 14-15 | Psalm 77 |
| 8 | John 12:27-50 | 2 Chronicles 16-17 | Psalm 78:1-20 |
| 9 | John 13:1-20 | 2 Chronicles 18 | Psalm 78:21-37 |
| 10 | John 13:21-38 | 2 Chronicles 19 | Psalm 78:38-55 |
| 11 | John 14:1-14 | 2 Chronicles 20:1-21:1 | Psalm 78:56-72 |
| 12 | John 14:15-31 | 2 Chronicles 21:2-22:12 | Psalm 79 |
| 13 | John 15:1-16:4a | 2 Chronicles 23 | Psalm 80 |
| 14 | John 16:4b-33 | 2 Chronicles 24 | Psalm 81 |
| 15 | John 17 | 2 Chronicles 25 | Psalm 82 |
| 16 | John 18:1-18 | 2 Chronicles 26 | Psalm 83 |
| 17 | John 18:19-38 | 2 Chronicles 27-28 | Psalm 84 |
| 18 | John 18:38b-19:16 | 2 Chronicles 29 | Psalm 85 |
| 19 | John 19:16-42 | 2 Chronicles 30 | Psalm 86 |
| 20 | John 20:1-18 | 2 Chronicles 31 | Psalm 87 |

| | | | |
|---|---|---|---|
| 21 | John 20:19-31 | 2 Chronicles 32 | Psalm 88 |
| 22 | John 21 | 2 Chronicles 33 | Psalm 89:1-18 |
| 23 | 1 John 1 | 2 Chronicles 34 | Psalm 89:19-37 |
| 24 | 1 John 2 | 2 Chronicles 35 | Psalm 89:38-52 |
| 25 | 1 John 3 | 2 Chronicles 36 | Psalm 90 |
| 26 | 1 John 4 | Ezra 1-2 | Psalm 91 |
| 27 | 1 John 5 | Ezra 3-4 | Psalm 92 |
| 28 | 2 John | Ezra 5-6 | Psalm 93 |
| 29 | 3 John | Ezra 7-8 | Psalm 94 |
| 30 | Jude | Ezra 9-10 | Psalm 95 |

## October

| | | | |
|---|---|---|---|
| 1 | Revelation 1 | Nehemiah 1-2 | Psalm 96 |
| 2 | Revelation 2 | Nehemiah 3 | Psalm 97 |
| 3 | Revelation 3 | Nehemiah 4 | Psalm 98 |
| 4 | Revelation 4 | Nehemiah 5:1-7:4 | Psalm 99 |
| 5 | Revelation 5 | Nehemiah 7:5-8:12 | Psalm 100 |
| 6 | Revelation 6 | Nehemiah 8:13-9:37 | Psalm 101 |
| 7 | Revelation 7 | Nehemiah 9:38-10:39 | Psalm 102 |
| 8 | Revelation 8 | Nehemiah 11 | Psalm 103 |
| 9 | Revelation 9 | Nehemiah 12 | Psalm 104:1-23 |
| 10 | Revelation 10 | Nehemiah 13 | Psalm 104:24-35 |
| 11 | Revelation 11 | Esther 1 | Psalm 105:1-25 |
| 12 | Revelation 12 | Esther 2 | Psalm 105:26-45 |
| 13 | Revelation 13 | Esther 3-4 | Psalm 106:1-23 |
| 14 | Revelation 14 | Esther 5:1-6:13 | Psalm 106:24-48 |
| 15 | Revelation 15 | Esther 6:14-8:17 | Psalm 107:1-22 |
| 16 | Revelation 16 | Esther 9-10 | Psalm 107:23-43 |
| 17 | Revelation 17 | Isaiah 1-2 | Psalm 108 |
| 18 | Revelation 18 | Isaiah 3-4 | Psalm 109:1-19 |
| 19 | Revelation 19 | Isaiah 5-6 | Psalm 109:20-31 |
| 20 | Revelation 20 | Isaiah 7-8 | Psalm 110 |
| 21 | Revelation 21-22 | Isaiah 9-10 | Psalm 111 |
| 22 | 1 Thessalonians 1 | Isaiah 11-13 | Psalm 112 |
| 23 | 1 Thessalonians 2:1-16 | Isaiah 14-16 | Psalm 113 |
| 24 | 1 Thessalonians 2:17-3:13 | Isaiah 17-19 | Psalm 114 |
| 25 | 1 Thessalonians 4 | Isaiah 20-22 | Psalm 115 |
| 26 | 1 Thessalonians 5 | Isaiah 23-24 | Psalm 116 |
| 27 | 2 Thessalonians 1 | Isaiah 25-26 | Psalm 117 |
| 28 | 2 Thessalonians 2 | Isaiah 27-28 | Psalm 118 |
| 29 | 2 Thessalonians 3 | Isaiah 29-30 | Psalm 119:1-32 |
| 30 | 1 Timothy 1 | Isaiah 31-33 | Psalm 119:33-64 |
| 31 | 1 Timothy 2 | Isaiah 34-35 | Psalm 119:65-96 |

## November

| | | | |
|---|---|---|---|
| 1 | 1 Timothy 3 | Isaiah 36-37 | Psalm 119:97-120 |
| 2 | 1 Timothy 4 | Isaiah 38-39 | Psalm 119:121-144 |
| 3 | 1 Timothy 5:1-22 | Jeremiah 1-2 | Psalm 119:145-176 |
| 4 | 1 Timothy 5:23-6:21 | Jeremiah 3-4 | Psalm 120 |
| 5 | 2 Timothy 1 | Jeremiah 5-6 | Psalm 121 |
| 6 | 2 Timothy 2 | Jeremiah 7-8 | Psalm 122 |
| 7 | 2 Timothy 3 | Jeremiah 9-10 | Psalm 123 |
| 8 | 2 Timothy 4 | Jeremiah 11-12 | Psalm 124 |
| 9 | Titus 1 | Jeremiah 13-14 | Psalm 125 |
| 10 | Titus 2 | Jeremiah 15-16 | Psalm 126 |
| 11 | Titus 3 | Jeremiah 17-18 | Psalm 127 |
| 12 | Philemon | Jeremiah 19-20 | Psalm 128 |
| 13 | James 1 | Jeremiah 21-22 | Psalm 129 |
| 14 | James 2 | Jeremiah 23-24 | Psalm 130 |
| 15 | James 3 | Jeremiah 25-26 | Psalm 131 |
| 16 | James 4 | Jeremiah 27-28 | Psalm 132 |
| 17 | James 5 | Jeremiah 29-30 | Psalm 133 |
| 18 | 1 Peter 1 | Jeremiah 31-32 | Psalm 134 |
| 19 | 1 Peter 2 | Jeremiah 33-34 | Psalm 135 |
| 20 | 1 Peter 3 | Jeremiah 35-36 | Psalm 136 |
| 21 | 1 Peter 4 | Jeremiah 37-38 | Psalm 137 |
| 22 | 1 Peter 5 | Jeremiah 39-40 | Psalm 138 |
| 23 | 2 Peter 1 | Jeremiah 41-42 | Psalm 139 |
| 24 | 2 Peter 2 | Jeremiah 43-44 | Psalm 140 |
| 25 | 2 Peter 3 | Jeremiah 45-46 | Psalm 141 |
| 26 | Galatians 1 | Jeremiah 47-48 | Psalm 142 |
| 27 | Galatians 2 | Jeremiah 49-50 | Psalm 143 |
| 28 | Galatians 3:1-18 | Jeremiah 51-52 | Psalm 144 |
| 29 | Galatians 3:19-4:20 | Lamentations 1-2 | Psalm 145 |
| 30 | Galatians 4:21-31 | Lamentations 3-4 | Psalm 146 |

## December

| | | | |
|---|---|---|---|
| 1 | Galatians 5:1-15 | Lamentations 5 | Psalm 147 |
| 2 | Galatians 5:16-26 | Ezekiel 1 | Psalm 148 |
| 3 | Galatians 6 | Ezekiel 2-3 | Psalm 149 |
| 4 | Ephesians 1 | Ezekiel 4-5 | Psalm 150 |
| 5 | Ephesians 2 | Ezekiel 6-7 | Isaiah 40 |
| 6 | Ephesians 3 | Ezekiel 8-9 | Isaiah 41 |
| 7 | Ephesians 4:1-16 | Ezekiel 10-11 | Isaiah 42 |
| 8 | Ephesians 4:17-32 | Ezekiel 12-13 | Isaiah 43 |
| 9 | Ephesians 5:1-20 | Ezekiel 14-15 | Isaiah 44 |
| 10 | Ephesians 5:21-33 | Ezekiel 16 | Isaiah 45 |

| | | | |
|---|---|---|---|
| 11 | Ephesians 6 | Ezekiel 17 | Isaiah 46 |
| 12 | Philippians 1:1-11 | Ezekiel 18 | Isaiah 47 |
| 13 | Philippians 1:12-30 | Ezekiel 19 | Isaiah 48 |
| 14 | Philippians 2:1-11 | Ezekiel 20 | Isaiah 49 |
| 15 | Philippians 2:12-30 | Ezekiel 21-22 | Isaiah 50 |
| 16 | Philippians 3 | Ezekiel 23 | Isaiah 51 |
| 17 | Philippians 4 | Ezekiel 24 | Isaiah 52 |
| 18 | Colossians 1:1-23 | Ezekiel 25-26 | Isaiah 53 |
| 19 | Colossians 1:24-2:19 | Ezekiel 27-28 | Isaiah 54 |
| 20 | Colossians 2:20-3:17 | Ezekiel 29-30 | Isaiah 55 |
| 21 | Colossians 3:18-4:18 | Ezekiel 31-32 | Isaiah 56 |
| 22 | Luke 1:1-25 | Ezekiel 33 | Isaiah 57 |
| 23 | Luke 1:26-56 | Ezekiel 34 | Isaiah 58 |
| 24 | Luke 1:57-80 | Ezekiel 35-36 | Isaiah 59 |
| 25 | Luke 2:1-20 | Ezekiel 37 | Isaiah 60 |
| 26 | Luke 2:21-52 | Ezekiel 38-39 | Isaiah 61 |
| 27 | Luke 3:1-20 | Ezekiel 40-41 | Isaiah 62 |
| 28 | Luke 3:21-38 | Ezekiel 42-43 | Isaiah 63 |
| 29 | Luke 4:1-30 | Ezekiel 44-45 | Isaiah 64 |
| 30 | Luke 4:31-44 | Ezekiel 46-47 | Isaiah 65 |
| 31 | Luke 5:1-26 | Ezekiel 48 | Isaiah 66 |

*"The Bible is the sheet-anchor of our liberties."*
U. S. Grant

*"In all my perplexities and distresses, the Bible has never failed to give me light and strength."*
Robert E. Lee

# PATRIOT PRESS

Patriot Press is proud to publish books that emphasize traditional American values. Our high standards insure good, wholesome content that is both educational and inspirational. For more information, visit: www.patriotpressbooks.com

*Books published by Patriot Press are created and printed in the United States of America.*

Layout and design by Michael Aubrecht/Pinstripe Press
www.pinstripepress.net

www.ingramcontent.com/pod-product-compliance
Lightning Source LLC
Chambersburg PA
CBHW072003090426
42740CB00011B/2069

* 9 7 8 0 9 7 9 6 0 0 0 1 2 *